Making Peg Dolls

Over 60 fun, creative projects for children and adults

Hawthorn Press

Published by Hawthorn Press, Hawthorn House, 1 Lansdown Lane, Stroud, Gloucestershire, GL5 1BJ, UK
Tel: (01453) 757040
E-mail: info@hawthornpress.com
Website: www.hawthornpress.com

Cover photograph © Margaret and Paul Bloom
Photographs by Paul Bloom
Illustrations by Margaret Bloom
Design by Lucy Guenot

Printed in China by Everbest Printing Company Limited 2016.
Printed on environmentally friendly paper manufactured from renewable forest stock.

Every effort has been made to trace the ownership of all copyrighted material. If any omission has been made, please bring this to the publisher's attention so that proper acknowledgement may be given in future editions.

The views expressed in this book are not necessarily those of the publisher.

Hardback edition first published 2012.
Paperback edition first published 2016.

British Library Cataloguing in Publication Data applied for.

ISBN 978-1-907359-77-4

For Paul, Samuel and Lev, my deepest love, always...

...Goldie got out her paints and carefully mixed a flesh color for the doll. She covered its face, neck, and ears, its arms and hands with the rosy tan paint, and waited for it to dry... Then she painted a little gleaming black eye on either side of the doll's nose and finally, holding it firmly around the waist with one hand, Goldie smiled and smiled into the doll's eyes in the friendliest, sweetest way, and she painted a smile right back to herself on the little doll's face.

From *Goldie the Dollmaker* by M. B. Goffstein

SAFETY NOTE
The toys in this book have been designed for handling by children aged three years and above. All materials used to make the toys should be checked for safety and labeled as non-toxic. All loose parts should be carefully glued or otherwise attached to the dolls, and younger children should be supervised to avoid choking if dolls (or other small pieces associated with the dolls) are placed in the mouth.

DISCLAIMER
The author and publisher cannot accept any legal responsibility or liability for accidents or damage arising from the use of any items mentioned in this book or in the carrying out of any of the projects.

Making Peg Dolls

Over 60 fun, creative projects for children and adults

Margaret Bloom

Photography by Paul Bloom

Hawthorn Press

Contents

Autumn

Winter

Tell me a story

Foreword

Just as healthy food can nourish a child's growing body, healthy play environments and healthy toys can nourish a child's budding soul. Of course, this begs the question – what is a healthy toy for children? In my long-term experience as a children's educator, I would claim that an over-riding principle of a 'healthy' toy is that it allows involvement and activity by the child.

This book is a wonderful example of such creative and active involvement. Each chapter opens a new imaginative window. The book journeys through the four seasons, but also takes time to include a variety of multi-cultural festivals, from Easter to Hanukkah to Japanese Children's Day. The patterns are simple and easy to follow, and the finished peg dolls call out to be held and played with.

A refreshing discovery for the adult reader is that the peg dolls are calling out to us as well as to the children! For those adults who feel they are drowning in the current 'consumer culture' that is so prevalent in our modern times, for those who feel overwhelmed by the excess stimulation of the technological world, this book offers a lifeboat through the very nature of its simplicity.

As a storyteller and storywriter, my delight with each chapter in this book lies in the possibility of new stories created by children and adults through playing with such simple toys or 'props'. The simpler the props the more the children's imaginations are left free to do the work (another principle of a healthy toy for children!).

Simple story props have a magical role to play in our modern life, where constant distractions seem to be pulling us from pillar to post. For those receiving a story, props such as these peg dolls can help arouse curiosity; they can help listening and concentration; they can encourage creative play; they can help carry a therapeutic message. For storytellers, props can help the teller remember the sequence of the story; they can help develop the confidence of a new storyteller; they can add artistic dimensions to the storytelling.

Most importantly, using props like these simple peg dolls can be enjoyable and fun for both the storyteller and the story listeners. In fact, the enjoyment I have had in writing this foreword has helped birth a little story...

Once upon a time there was a family of wooden pegs who were not happy with sitting all day long in a straight row on a washing line. They knew they were born for greater things. This family of wooden pegs lived in a garden where children played all day, and the pegs wanted to play as well...

Thank you Margaret Bloom for helping the peg family to find their creative calling! And thank you for offering us, the readers, whether adult or child or both, a creative journey of our own.

Susan Perrow (M.Ed.)
www.healingthroughstories.com

Introduction

If you visit my home, you might notice a wee sprite (or two) peeking out from behind my teapot. If you look carefully among my books, it's possible to observe the tiny family of gnomes which has taken up residence. And all along my window sills are perched flutters of fairies, chirpy little bluebirds and two diminutive owls hooting softly.

In December 2010 I painted my first peg doll and was so delighted with the result that I wanted to paint more. My son and I painted handfuls of them to play with, and I continued to paint yet more little dolls to give away as gifts. I encouraged my friends to try this new favorite craft and the results were enchanting. Now I invite you to open yourself to the inspiration these tiny dolls can bring.

Within this book you will find over 60 different designs and patterns for peg dolls. I hope you enjoy creating them as much as I have enjoyed dreaming them up for you! And please do not limit yourself to my designs. Give a handful of blank dolls (along with some pencils and paint) to your eager children and see what they come up with. Hold a few dolls in your own hands. Let them whisper into your ear their own stories. Each little doll has a story to tell...

Margaret Bloom

Introducing the Craft of Peg Dolls

A friend was recently telling me that, when she sees peg dolls, she imagines a child in prehistoric times picking up a stick, wrapping it in a leaf or a bit of fur and gently cradling it. Perhaps, way back in those prehistoric times, an adult saw the nurturing instinct and carved a face on the stick for the child to love. Even now, when we watch children immersed in imaginative play, and one child presents us with a bit of wood saying, 'This is my baby,' these imaginings of children at play cross the expanses of history and cultures to connect us in a universal way.

Akin to a child's instinct to cradle simple sticks wrapped in leaves, peg dolls were first created from utilitarian laundry pegs. Many countries, too, have, in their unique traditions, doll designs which closely relate to peg dolls. In Japan, for example, beautiful Kokeshi dolls are distinctly peg doll-like.

In the handcraft tradition of Waldorf education from Germany, the legs of clothes pegs were removed to create small wooden bases on which dolls could be designed. These little dolls have traditionally been crafted into seasonal figures for nature table displays and imaginative play within home and classroom. A distinctive aspect of Waldorf peg doll design is the custom of leaving the faces of dolls unpainted. The idea behind this is to offer children an opportunity to project features and emotions onto the dolls. This, in turn, may create further possibility for imaginative and emotional development.

I've chosen to paint small, neutral faces on my dolls, and in designing your own dolls this is one of many design choices you can make. It might be your wish to leave the faces of your dolls unpainted, to paint simple, neutral features or to create faces which appear more animated.

Another distinctive aspect of traditional peg dolls is that they usually lack arms and hands. Again, the feeling behind this is that, whether the doll actually has hands or not, a child playing with the doll will imagine them there. One can find examples of peg dolls with a bit of pipe-cleaner or chenille wire secured around the body to create arms. However, in creating play-things for children, I appreciate the simplicity and durability of plain peg dolls. Another solution, however, for adding hands is to paint them onto the body of your doll. You can see a lovely example in the photo below.

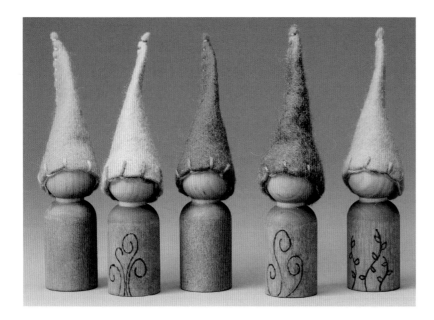

Although the dolls in this book appear to be fragile and made for display, they are actually of sturdy construction. Everything is sewn or glued securely and the dolls are made to be played with – even my toddler has his own peg doll 'babies' (I was ever so pleased when I found 9 cm (3½ in) doll-bases – they make marvellous baby toys).

During play, dolls might get damaged, but they are easily repaired. One of my favorite peg doll stories concerns the fate of a tiny sprite I sent to a friend in Australia. The little doll was immediately adopted by Alice, the two-year-old daughter of my friend. Alice loved the tiny sprite, played with it for hours and then tucked it into the pocket of her skirt. Alice's skirt went into the laundry and my friend apologetically related to me the resulting sad state of the doll. The wool felt hat and wings of the doll were unrecognizably misshapen and the paint of the poor doll's face, gown and hair were rather faded. I told my friend that there was no need to apologize; paint can easily be retouched and a new hat sewn. Inside, I smiled to hear what had happened to this little doll because I knew the work of my hands had been played with and loved.

When a child is given a toy created by the hands of someone who loves them, it holds special meaning. As an adult, looking at my creations, I sometimes worry I have painted the eyes unevenly or sewn an untidy seam, but no matter. Every doll I've made for a child has been adored. When making your own dolls, I hope you will enjoy the process and create dolls in your own, unique style. The patterns in this book for making peg dolls are laid out clearly; however, my instructions should be regarded as mere suggestions rather than prescriptive directions. Choose your own colors, add ornamentation, create a new hat! The dolls made by your own hands will be loved by the children who play with them.

Even more delightful, however, are the dolls children create for themselves. It gives me such joy to observe my older son sitting down with a friend to paint up a few dolls and then to see them play with the toys

they've created for themselves. All children need are a few blank dolls, some pencils, paint and perhaps a bit of felt; I am always enchanted by the ideas and creativity of the children who sit at my table and make dolls.

Give a handful of blank dolls (along with some pencils and paint) to your eager children and see what they create. Hold a few dolls in your own hands. Let them whisper in your dreams. Each little doll has a story to tell...

Materials and Techniques

When setting out to create peg dolls, the supplies you will need are fairly basic. Except for the wooden peg doll bases, you might already have most of the required supplies in your craft cupboard and sewing box.

Peg Dolls and Other Wooden Pieces

I have used five different sized doll-bases for the projects in this book: 6 cm (2⅜ in) standard wood-people-pegs, 5 cm (2 in) angel-pegs, 4 cm (1⅝ in) boy-pegs, 3 cm (1³⁄₁₆ in) baby/bee-shape pegs and 3 cm (1³⁄₁₆ in) tot-pegs. There is a resource guide at the back of this book listing places where you can purchase peg doll bases as well as wooden candle-cups for the Hanukkah project on page 151. If you have purchased doll-bases which do not match the sizes or shapes of the wooden bases I have used, you should be able to adjust my patterns and designs to fit your dolls. In addition to this, an alternative to purchasing 3 cm doll pegs would be to use a small hand-saw to remove approximately 1 cm from a boy-peg base.

Paint and Paint Brushes

I use a 12-tone watercolor pan set to paint my dolls, and I also keep on hand a few bottles of acrylic paint in basic tones – white, black, red, yellow, blue plus gold and silver for the occasional flourish. Depending on your personal preferences, any type of paint will do as long as it is non-toxic; more important are your paint brushes. I own many paint brushes but I only use two of them – a fine point round brush for painting small details and a slightly larger round brush for painting hair and clothes on the dolls. I purchased several high-quality paintbrushes nearly 20 years ago, and because I clean them immediately after use and don't leave them standing in water, they are still my favorites today.

Painting Skin-Surfaces

I like to leave the natural wood-grain showing on the faces of my doll. I have, however, seen many peg dolls where the faces were painted with a skin-tone before the facial features were applied. This is entirely a matter of preference and choice.

Painting Eyes

When you are painting eyes on your dolls you will want to be sure your paint is rather thick (not too diluted). Thinner paint can sometimes be drawn along the grain of the wood, creating a smudged effect, and there is also the risk that your paint will run if it is too watery.

Colored Pencils

Although I usually paint the faces of my dolls freehand, occasionally I want to be sure of eye placement. In these cases, I use a pencil to create small marks before applying paint. Other times, I might want to create a face with a softer look and so I leave the face drawn with pencil marks only. Drawing faces on the dolls with pencil is also a useful technique for any child who worries he might blot the face by using paint. It's much easier for school-age children to draw a face with precision using a pencil than to create a tiny face with paint.

Wool Felt

Wool felt comes in many gorgeous colors and has a fine texture which cannot be imitated by synthetics. It is more expensive than synthetic felt, but for these tiny doll projects you don't need very much. When I first started making peg dolls, I created at least 35 dolls using bits and scraps of felt from my stash before I decided I wanted more colors to work with. If wool felt is not available in your local shops, you can check the resource guide at the end of this book for a list of places where you can purchase it.

Cutting Felt

Even when cutting multiple pattern pieces identical in shape, you will want to cut each piece of felt individually. Because of the thickness of felt, it is difficult to cut small pieces of felt accurately when cutting more than one piece at a time.

Glue

Any type of thick, all-purpose, white craft glue which is non-toxic and clear-drying will work to attach felt hats and garments to your dolls. I would also like to caution you against using hot-glue. Standard white craft glue takes a few minutes to set and dry which will allow you the chance to reposition items if you choose. Because hot-glue dries very quickly it's difficult to make adjustments once items have been attached with it.

Embroidery Floss, Needles and Fabric Scissors

I use six-strand, cotton embroidery floss; it can be found in every color imaginable... For the seams and embroidery in this book, I use two strands of embroidery floss which I have separated from the six-ply strands. In addition to a good pair of fabric scissors, a set of pinking shears can come in handy for cutting little crowns and various embellishments.

Beeswax Polish

Using beeswax polish on your dolls is optional and a matter of taste. When watercolor paint dries on the wooden bases it will have soft matte finish. Giving your painted surfaces a good rub with beeswax polish will make the watercolor paint transparent so that the wood-grain shows through, and it will also give the surface a delicate sheen. I use a beeswax polish on dolls which will not be covered by felt garments, and I never use it on the faces of my dolls as it can sometimes cause the paint to smudge. To make your own polish, heat a small amount of beeswax in a double-boiler along with some jojoba or olive oil.

PATTERN TEMPLATES

All patterns for cutting felt pieces are represented in this book in their actual size. For the purposes of your own projects you may trace them or scan them and then print them out.

The usual ratio of beeswax to oil is 1:3 (the beeswax being the smaller amount). I prefer a ratio of 1:5, and you can certainly make adjustments to suit your own personal preferences. I made about 35 g (just over an ounce) of this polish many months ago and poured it off into a small glass jar. It keeps well, and because it's used in small amounts, there's no need to make large quantities. To apply the wax, place a small amount on a soft piece of cloth or paper towel. Rub the painted areas until no paint residue is visible on a clean section of cloth.

Wool Roving and a Notched Felting Needle

I have used wool roving on several projects in this book. Roving comes in many beautiful colors, is easy to work with, and is a nice way to add small details to doll designs (note: if you choose to use needle felting techniques on your doll costumes, always support your needle-felting work on a piece of thick foam to avoid stabbing yourself!). If you don't have felting supplies to hand, you can stitch or glue bits of yarn into place as a substitute for wool roving when creating dolls.

Extra Embellishments

Glitter, beads, bits of lace, tiny bells, feathers and seashells are lovely to have available as embellishments for your dolls. In addition to the supplies listed above, acorn caps make perfect hats for tiny dolls and paper flower-stamens make wonderful fairy antennae. You might also find that floral wire, chenille wire and craft paper can be useful. While none of these supplies are necessary for making peg dolls, a supply of small embellishments can be inspiring as you create costumes for your dolls.

Glossary of Stitches

This is a list of needle-stitches I have used on the projects in this book. There are many variations of embroidery stitches and, if you prefer, you could substitute other stitch designs for the ones I've suggested.

BLANKET STITCH
This stitch can be used to create a decorative edging or to attach two pieces of fabric together.

RUNNING STITCH
This basic stitch can be used to attach two pieces of fabric together or to create a gathered area.

FELL STITCH (ALSO REFERRED TO AS APPLIQUÉ STITCH)

This stitch can be used to create a flat seam where one piece of fabric is overlapping another (as in overlapping fabric to create a cone-shaped gnome hat). Fell stitch can also be used to attach a decorative piece of fabric onto a larger piece.

DAISY STITCH

1. Bring your needle through the fabric, from the wrong side to the right side, then reinsert your needle as close as possible to the spot where your thread is emerging. Before pulling the needle all the way through the fabric, push the tip back through (to the right side) at the point where you wish to anchor your daisy-petal loop.

2. As you pull the needle through to the right side of the fabric, wrap the thread under the needle so that the loop will be caught as you continue to pull the thread all the way through. Finish by anchoring your loop with a small stitch.

Step 1

Step 2

FRENCH KNOT
1. Bring your needle through the fabric, from the back. Starting near the center of your needle, wrap the thread towards the needle-tip.

2. Sliding the wrapped portions of thread toward the tip of the needle (and pulled taut), push the tip of the needle back into the fabric just next to where the thread came out.

3. Gently draw the thread through the wrapped portions, keeping the wrapped portions pressed close against the fabric as you pull.

STRAIGHT STITCH/STAR STITCH

COUCHING STITCH

Doodle Page

Here is a little space for you to draw and doodle. Perhaps you might like to experiment with how high or low you place the eyes on the faces of your dolls. Try inventing costumes for your dolls in a range of springtime colors and then sketch them again in a range of autumnal colors.

Go ahead, scribble away, have fun!

Chapter One

Spring

Spring Flowers

I love clustering these little spring flower-folk together like garden bouquets. I've created a grouping of snowdrops, buttercups and forget-me-nots...

And a nosegay of primroses and wild violets, too...

SUPPLIES

5 cm (2 in) angel-pegs

4 cm (1⅝ in) boy-pegs

3 cm (1³⁄₁₆ in) tot-pegs

Watercolor paint and brushes

Wool felt: white, pink, lavender, yellow, blue and green

Thin-gauge, fabric-wrapped floral wire

Matching embroidery floss and needles

Tracing paper or a photocopy of patterns

Fabric scissors

A pencil

Glue

Spring is coming, Spring is coming
Birdies build your nest.
Weave together straw and feather
Doing each your best,
Doing each your best.

Spring is coming, Spring is coming
Flowers are waking too,
Daisies, lilies, daffodillies,
All are coming through,
All are coming through.

Spring is coming, Spring is coming
All around is fair,
Shimmer, glimmer on the meadow,
Joy is everywhere,
Joy is everywhere!

Traditional

What flowers will you find growing in your garden this spring?

Painting the dolls

1. Using 5 cm (2 in) angel-pegs for the snow drops and primroses, 4 cm (1⅝ in) boy-pegs for violets and buttercups and 3 cm (1³/₁₆ in) tot-pegs for forget-me-nots, paint bodies of the dolls light green.

2. Paint the calyx-collars of the flowers in a darker green around the necks.

3. Add hair and faces.

Making the hats

4. Cut out the flower hat pieces. Overlap points A and B and stitch or glue in place.

5. Add embroidery and then glue hats in place on the doll heads.

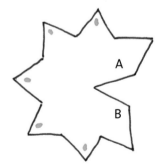

WHITE SNOWDROPS
Add a small stitch of green at the tip of each petal.

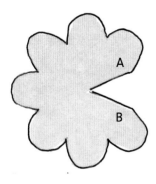

YELLOW BUTTERCUPS

In a slightly darker shade of yellow, add a circle of daisy stitches at the crown.

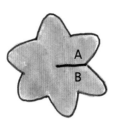

BLUE FORGET-ME-NOTS

Add a small circle of yellow stitching around the center of the crown at the top.

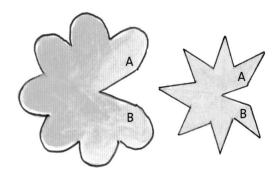

PRIMROSES

Glue additional felt piece together, point A to point B, and then glue this piece to the top of the hat.

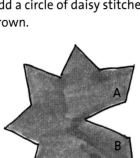

WILD VIOLETS

If you do a bit of research, you will find there are many types of wild violets. I like the ones with just a bit of yellow in the center, so when I created my violets, I simply added one stitch of yellow to the front.

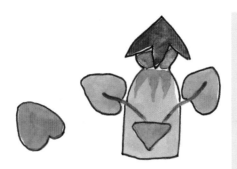

LEAVES

Though I could have added leaves to all these flower-fairies, I decided to only add them to the violets. If you choose to add leaves, you can simply glue the leaves directly to the bodies of your dolls. In the case of the violets, I made the leaves quite small and so thought they might look nice attached to stems. For the stems,

Pattern Templates

All patterns for cutting felt pieces are represented in this book in their actual size. For the purposes of your own projects you may trace them or scan them and then print them out.

I bent short pieces of floral wire (6 cm (2⅜ in) into a 'V' shape, glued the leaves onto the ends and then secured the 'V' of the floral wire to the backs of the dolls by gluing bits of felt over the wires.

Bluebirds

*Why, that's the blue bird we were looking for! ...We
went so far and he was here all the time!*

From *The Blue Bird* by Maurice Maeterlinck

When I was about five years old my mother took me to a screening of the 1940 movie *The Bluebird* starring Shirley Temple, based on the 1908 play by Maurice Maeterlinck. The story is about a brother and sister, Tyltyl and Mytyl, who are sent out by the fairy Berylune into magical realms to search for the Bluebird of Happiness. Returning home empty-handed, the children see that the bird has been in a cage in their home the whole time. When Tyltyl gives the bird as a gift to a neighbor's sick child, the bird escapes and flies away. In the end, the children learn that happiness can truly be found waiting within oneself.

SUPPLIES

6 cm (2³⁄₈ in) standard wood-people-peg

Wool felt: light blue and yellow

Matching embroidery floss and needles

Blue wool roving, a notched felting needle and thick foam block

Watercolor paint and brushes

Tracing paper or a photocopy of patterns

Fabric scissors

A pencil

Glue

Painting the dolls

1. Using a 6 cm (2³⁄₈ in) standard wood-people-peg paint the head and body a pale blue, leaving the chest and stomach unpainted, plus an unpainted oval for the face.

2. Paint a wee-birdie face.

3. Mix a reddish-pink tone of paint and, starting at the top of the chest, blend your reddish-pink paint downwards, shading into white as you reach the bottom of the doll-base.

Making the hats

4. Cut out front and back pieces of the hat according to the pattern and align along the top. Using two strands of matching embroidery floss, sew around the curved top of the hat.

Hat back

Hat front

5. Take a tiny wisp of blue wool roving to match your hat color. Fold the fibers of the roving in half and half again. Place the hat on a thick piece of foam and place your little fiber bundle on the pointed peak at the top of the hat. Then take your felting needle and start stabbing one end of your little fiber-bundle through the felt of little point on top of the hat. Between stabs, use your needle to pull straying wisps of fiber in towards the peaked portion of the hat where you are securing your fibers.

6. When you are satisfied that your fibers are secured, use sharp scissors to trim the fibers at the sides and across the top of the little wispy top-knot you've created for your bluebird. Alternately, if you don't have needle-felting materials on hand, you could stitch a fuzzy bit of yarn in place, add a bit of feather or leave the top of the hat plain (the little peak at the top of the hat is terribly cute, all on its own and unadorned!)

7. With two strands of matching embroidery floss, sew a running stitch along the bottom edge of the back of the hat and gather gently to fit the contour of the doll's head.

Felting needle

Wing

Beak

Adding wings

8. Glue the hat onto the doll and add the yellow beak piece to the front of the hat at the center.

9. Cut out the wings and glue them to the sides of the doll.

Purim

In Jewish synagogues throughout the world, the story of Esther is retold every year during the holiday of Purim in early March. The story tells of an evil advisor to Ahasu-e'rus, the king of Persia. This advisor, named Haman, bore a grudge against Mordechai, Esther's cousin, and so advised the king to exterminate all the Jewish people within his realm. Esther risked incurring the king's anger by revealing herself as Jewish and requesting he withdraw his edict to destroy her people. To this day, Esther is renowned for her act of bravery and for saving her fellow Jews. The celebration of Purim is a very joyous one; children dress up and parade in costume, sweet pastries called Hamantaschen (said to be in the shape of Haman's hat) are baked, and the story of Purim is re-enacted, either as a comical stage play or a puppet show.

These little peg dolls could be used to re-enact the story of Purim or any other story which tells of a brave queen and the triumph of good over evil.

Now there was a Jew in Shushan the capital whose name was Mordechai. He had brought up Hadassah, that is Esther, the daughter of his uncle, for she had neither father nor mother; the maiden was beautiful and lovely. So when the king's order and his edict were proclaimed, and when many maidens were gathered in Shushan the capital, Esther was also taken into the king's palace... And the maiden pleased him and won his favor. Esther had not made known her people or kindred for Mordechai had charged her not to make it known.

Esther 2:5-11

SUPPLIES

Four 5 cm (2 in) angel-pegs

Wool felt in a variety of colors

Matching embroidery floss and needles

A small amount of brown yarn

Embellishments such as beads, sequins and feathers

A notched felting needle and a thick foam block

Wool roving: brown, black and grey

Watercolor paint and brushes

Tracing paper or a photocopy of patterns

Fabric scissors and pinking shears

Glue

ESTHER

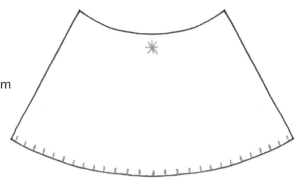

Painting the doll

1. Paint hair and a face on a 5 cm (2 in) angel-peg.

Dress

Crown

Dressing the doll

2. From white felt, cut out the dress-piece, add embroidery (if you wish) and then glue the dress around the body, carefully smoothing the felt to fit the contours of the wooden doll-base. Trim off any extra felt at the back if necessary.

Adding hair and a crown

3. To make the crown, use pinking-shears to clip a narrow piece of felt, approximately 6 cm (2³⁄₈ in) in a bright yellow or golden color and glue the crown around the head of your doll. If you'd like to add a plait, braid three pieces of yarn or embroidery floss to match the hair you've painted on the doll. Secure one end of the plait with a bit of embroidery floss (I used golden floss) and secure the other end of the plait beneath the crown when you glue it into place around the doll's head.

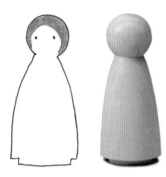

KING AHASU-E'RUS

Painting the doll

1. Paint hair and eyes on a 5 cm (2 in) angel-peg.

Dressing the doll

2. Cut the tunic, cloak, belt and crown pieces from felt. Glue the tunic over the front of the doll's body, add a bit of embroidery to the belt if you wish (I used a simple couching stitch) and then secure the belt in place with a bit of glue. To finish off dressing your doll, wrap the cloak around the back and sides of the doll and glue in place.

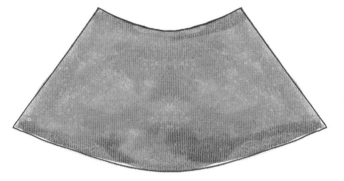

Tunic

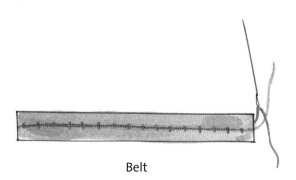

Belt

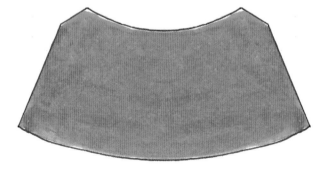

Cloak

Creating the crown

3. To create the crown for King Ahasu-e'rus, stitch your two A pieces together over the curved top and glue onto the head of your doll. Then take piece B and glue around the A pieces. For a bit of sparkle and panache, add a sequin, glitter or feathers to the crown of your king.

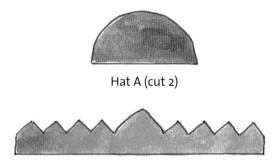

Hat A (cut 2)

Hat B

Adding a beard

4. To create a beard for your doll, take a few wisps of wool roving (for King Ahasu-e'rus, I overlaid a bit of light brown roving with a bit of darker brown) and fold the fibers in half. Place your fibers on a piece of thick foam, give them a few stabs across the folded area with your felting-needle and then, with the tip of your needle, start pulling in stray fibers from the sides and over the top. Keep stabbing and pulling in bits of stray fiber until you have a more densely felted area at the top and wisps of unfelted beard hanging down. Finally, trim your beard across the top (if necessary) and sides to neaten things up. You can also trim and shape the beard along the bottom edge, if you wish. When you are satisfied with the shape of the beard, glue it onto the lower portion of the face of your doll.

Alternatively, if you don't want to needle-felt a beard, you could use a few wisps of unfelted roving or bits of yarn to create a beard for your doll. And yet another way to make a beard would be to cut a small piece of brown, grey or black felt into shape and glue it on the face of your doll.

HAMAN

Painting the doll

1. Paint hair and eyes on a 5 cm (2 in) angel-peg.

Dressing the doll

2. Cut the tunic, cloak, belt and hat pieces from felt. Glue the tunic over the front of the doll's body, add a bit of embroidery to the belt if you wish (I used a couching stitch) and then secure the belt in place with a bit of glue. To finish off dressing your doll, wrap the cloak around the back of the doll and glue in place.

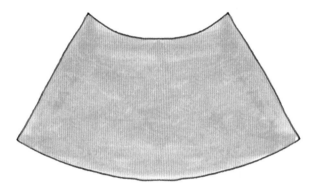

Tunic

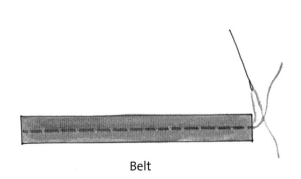

Belt

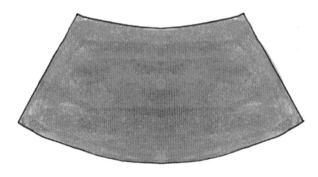

Cloak

Creating the hat

3. To create Haman's hat (in the shape of a hamantaschen, of course!) glue the small triangle (B) or use an appliqué fell stitch to attach it onto one of your A pieces. Then, using a blanket stitch, sew your two A pieces together over the tall, pointed top. When you are done sewing, glue the hat onto the head of your doll.

Hat A (cut 2)

Hat B

Adding a beard

4. To create a beard for Haman, see page 38 under instructions for King Ahasu-e'rus.

MORDECHAI

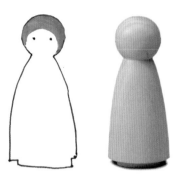

Painting the doll

1. Paint hair and eyes on a 5 cm (2 in) angel-peg.

Dressing the doll

2. Cut the tunic, cloak and hat pieces from felt. Glue the tunic over the front of the doll's body, then wrap the cloak around the back of the doll and glue in place.

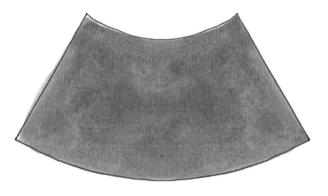

Tunic

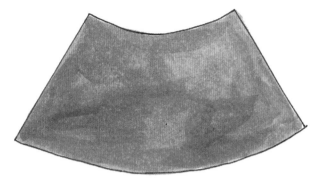

Cloak

Creating the hat

3. To create Mordechai's hat, cut two pieces according to the pattern and, using a blanket stitch, sew the two pieces together. Then glue the hat onto the head of the doll.

Hat

Adding a beard

4. To create a beard for Mordechai, see page 38 under instructions for King Ahasu-e'rus.

Japanese Hinamatsuri

Let's light the lanterns on the tiered stand,

Let's arrange the peach blossom branches.

Five court musicians are playing flutes and drums.

Today is a joyful Dolls' Festival.

Traditional song

SUPPLIES

Two 6 cm (2⅜ in) standard wood-people-pegs

Three 4 cm (1⅝ in) boy-pegs

Wool felt in a variety of colors: pink, peach, red, yellow and greens

Matching embroidery floss and needles

A toothpick

Watercolor paint and brushes

Fabric scissors

Tracing paper or a photocopy of patterns

A pencil

Glue

Hinamatsuri (translated as Dolls' Festival and also referred to as Girls' Day) is celebrated in Japan on March 3rd. For this festival, families bring out a special set of dolls dressed in traditional court costumes of the Heian period (795-1185) and set them on red, tiered platforms. Most families only set out the top tier with the Emperor and Empress dolls, and sometimes the next tier with three saké-bearing court attendants. In a full set, the Emperor and Empress sit at the top, and on the various rows below them are the attendants, musicians, court ministers and samurai, plus an elaborate array of symbolic foods, flowers, trees and decorative furnishings.

I've created a *Hinamatsuri* display with an Emperor and Empress, their three attendants plus traditional lanterns and branches of peach blossoms. Sitting on their tiered platforms, these little figures are all ready to celebrate a joyful Dolls' Festival!

THE EMPEROR

Painting the doll

1. Paint hair and a face on a 6 cm (2³⁄₈ in) standard wood-people-peg.

2. Paint the body a pale cream color.

Dressing the doll

3. Glue the trousers around the lower portion of the body.

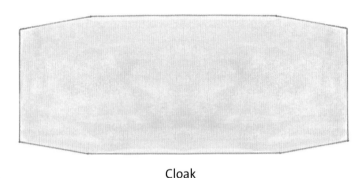

Cloak

4. Cut the cloak pattern-piece twice, once from a darker green felt to match the doll's trousers and the second piece in a lighter green color. Glue or stitch these two pieces together and apply a bit more glue to the darker under-cloak. Then wrap the outer robes around the 'shoulders' of the doll, securing in front with a stitch or two of embroidery thread.

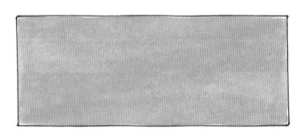

Trousers

Creating the hat

5. To make the Emperor's hat, cut out two hat pieces, stitch together over the top and glue onto the head of the doll.

Hat

6. For the decorative cross-piece, trim a length of skewer or toothpick to 2.5 cm (1 in), paint it black and then sew in place onto the hat.

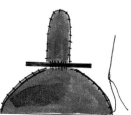

Baton

7. Traditionally, the Emperor holds a ritual baton called a Shaku in his right hand. To add a Shaku to your Emperor, cut the baton from felt according to the pattern and glue in place.

THE EMPRESS

Painting the doll

1. Paint hair and a face on a 6 cm (2⅜ in) standard wood-people-peg.

2. Paint the lower ¾ of the doll body a dark red and the upper section in white. To create the illusion of the wrapped under-layers of her garb, you can use a pencil to draw a 'y' shape beneath the neck of the doll (on the area which has been painted white).

Dressing the doll

3. Cut out the cloak-piece twice, once from a dark red felt to match the doll's skirt and the second piece in a pale pink color. Glue or stitch these two pieces together and apply a bit more glue to the darker under-cloak. Then wrap the outer robes around the 'shoulders' of the doll, securing in front with a stitch or two of matching embroidery thread.

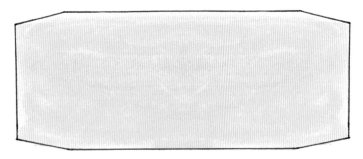

Cloak

Adding the crown and fan

4. Traditionally, the Empress holds a fan and wears a decorative hair ornament with three small points. To add these to your doll, cut felt according to the pattern pieces and glue into place.

SAKÉ-BEARING COURT ATTENDANTS

Painting the doll

1. Paint hair and a faces on three 4 cm (1⅝ in) boy-pegs.

2. Paint the lower ¾ of the doll body a dark red and the upper section in white. To create the illusion of the wrapped under layers of the traditional garb, you can use a pencil to draw a 'y' shape beneath the neck of the doll (on the area which has been painted white).

Dressing the doll

3. Cut out the cloak-piece twice, once from a dark red felt to match the doll's skirt and the second piece in a pale peach color. Glue or stitch these two pieces together and apply a bit more glue to the darker under-cloak. Then wrap the outer robes around the 'shoulders' of the doll, securing in front with a stitch or two of matching embroidery thread.

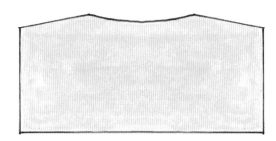

Cloak

Crown

Ornaments and implements

4. Traditionally, the attendants wear smaller decorative hair ornaments than the empress but in a similar design.

Each attendant will also be carrying implements for serving saké. The doll to the right holds a long-handled serving cup, the doll on the left holds a pot of saké and the center doll carries a tray with a serving cup. To add these items to your dolls, cut felt according to the shapes of the pattern pieces and glue into place.

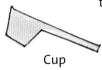

Cup

Pot of saké

Tray with cup

ADDITIONAL ITEMS

Traditionally, the dolls are set up on red, tiered platforms. I've created platforms from toy building blocks which I've covered with red paper. The Emperor and Empress are always seated on small ornamental straw mats placed on their platform; I've made these mats out of paper. Additionally, it is usual to have a gold or decorative screen behind the emperor and empress, plus white lanterns and branches of peach blossoms which symbolize gentility, composure, tranquility and a happy marriage.

Japanese Children's Day

Higher than the roof-tops are the koinobori

The large carp is the father,

The smaller carp are children,

They are enjoying swimming in the sky.

Traditional song

Children's Day (*Kodomo No Hi* in Japanese) observed on May 5th, celebrates all children. For this holiday, families fly flags called *koinobori* in the shape of carp because, symbolically, carp represent strength and success in life. While *koinobori* are usually flown from tall flagpoles, occasionally children will have smaller versions trailing at the end of short sticks. I have dressed my little peg dolls in traditional kimono and given each a small, fluttering *koinobori* for their Children's Day celebration.

SUPPLIES

Several 4 cm (1⅝ in) boy-pegs

Wool felt: dark blue, brown, pink (or any other colors you might choose)

Watercolor paint, gold paint and brushes

Toothpicks

Small wooden beads

Colorful paper

Fabric scissors

A pencil

A ruler

Glue

Painting the dolls

1. Using 4 cm (1⅝ in) boy-pegs, paint hair and faces.

2. Paint the bodies of your dolls. When the paint is dry, you may rub it with beeswax polish to create a deeper tone and a soft sheen (optional).

Creating the *Obi* waist sashes

Sash

3. To form the *obi* (traditional waist sashes), cut 2 strips of felt in colors contrasting with the painted doll bodies.Each strip should be 6 cm (2¼ in) long by 7 mm (¼ in) wide. The first strip is glued around the body to form the waist sash and the second strip should be folded to form a loop and then glued to the back of the doll.

Making the *Koinobori*

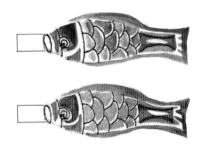

4. I've drawn and painted some tiny, *koinobori* for my *Kodomo No Hi* peg dolls. Here are some *koinobori* which you can copy and cut out for your dolls if you wish. To make the poles from which they flutter, I glued small, wooden beads to the tops of toothpicks and painted the beads gold. Then I glued the *koinobori* below the gold wooden beads and added fluttering paper streamers which often accompany the pretty flying fish.

Making *Kabuto* helmets

Another tradition for *Kodomo No Hi* is to display small models of *kabuto* (traditional Japanese military helmets) or fold small *kabuto* from origami paper.

I folded origami *kabuto* helmets to fit 6 cm (2⅜ in) standard wood-people-pegs. Here are instructions to fold your own little helmets. (Note: All folds should be creased sharply).

1. Start with a small square of colorful origami paper measuring 7 cm (2¾ in) on all sides. With the white side of the paper facing up, fold the square corner-to-corner so that you end up with a triangle. The colorful side of the paper should now be visible on the outside of the triangle.

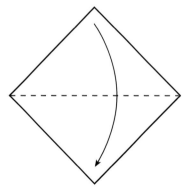

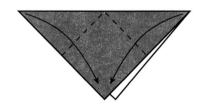

2. Bring each of the top corners down to meet the bottom point.

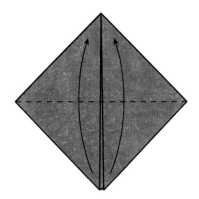

3. Fold the top layer flaps upward (in half) to meet at the top point.

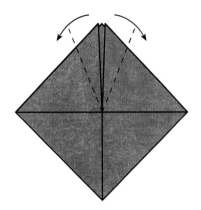

4. Fold the corners of the top layer outward along the crease-lines as indicated.

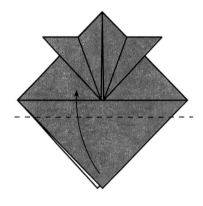

5. Fold the top layer upwards along the crease-line as indicated.

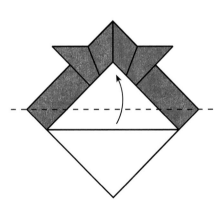

6. Fold the lower edge upwards again to form the edging of the helmet.

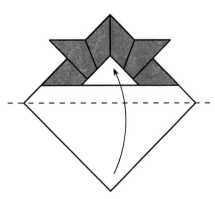

7. Fold the bottom flap upwards and inside the hat. Crease neatly along the edge of the fold.

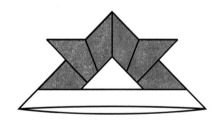

8. Now your doll has a hat and is ready to celebrate Children's Day!

Easter

On Easter morn at early dawn
before the cocks were crowing
I met a bob-tail bunnykin
and asked where he was going.
'Tis in the house and out the house
a-tipsy, tipsy-toeing,
Tis round the house and 'bout the house
a-lightly I am going.'
'But what is that of every hue
you carry in your basket?'
'Tis eggs of gold and eggs of blue;
I wonder that you ask it.'

'Tis chocolate eggs and bonbon eggs
and eggs of red and gray,
For every child in every house
on bonny Easter day.'
He perked his ears and winked his eye
and twitched his little nose;
He shook his tail—what tail he had—
and stood up on his toes.
'I must be gone before the sun;
the east is growing gray;
Tis almost time for bells to chime.'
So he hippety-hopped away.

Rowena Bennett

SUPPLIES

Two 6 cm (2³⁄₈ in) standard wood-people-pegs
Several 3 cm (1³⁄₁₆ in) tot-pegs
Wool felt: white, grey, red and yellow
Matching embroidery floss and needles
Watercolor paint and brushes
Fabric scissors
Tracing paper or a photocopy of patterns
A pencil
Glue

RABBIT

Painting the doll

1. Using a 6 cm (2⅜ in) standard wood-people-peg, paint the body and head grey (or brown or white, according to your preference) leaving an unpainted circle or oval for the face.

2. Paint the face.

Making the hat

3. Cut out front and back pieces according to the pattern and align the ears. Using two strands of matching embroidery floss, sew around the top of the hat and ears using a blanket stitch.

4. If you would like to be able to bend the ears, take a 5 cm (2 in) piece of wired chenille, bend it into a 'U' shape and insert ends of the wire into the ears.

Rabbit hat (back)

Rabbit hat (front)

5. With two strands of matching embroidery floss, sew a running-stitch along the bottom of the back of the hat and gather slightly to fit the contour of the doll's head.

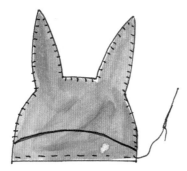

6. Glue the hat onto the head.

The finishing touch

7. Cut out and then glue the oval stomach-piece to the front of the doll.

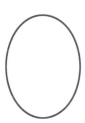

Rabbit stomach

MAMA HEN

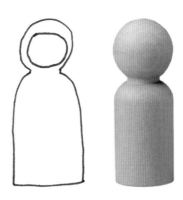

Painting the doll

1. Using a 6 cm (2³⁄₈ in) standard wood-people-peg, paint the body and head white, leaving a circle or unpainted oval for the face.

2. Paint the face.

Covering the body

3. Using two strands of white embroidery floss, sew a running stitch along one side of the white felt body piece and gather slightly to fit the contour around the neck of the doll.

4. Apply a small amount of glue to the inside of the felt body piece and glue it to the doll with the opening in the back.

5. With two strands of white embroidery floss, use an overcast stitch to sew up the back.

Making the hat

6. Cut front and back hat pieces from wool felt. Align the hat pieces and then, using two strands of matching embroidery floss, sew around the top of the hat.

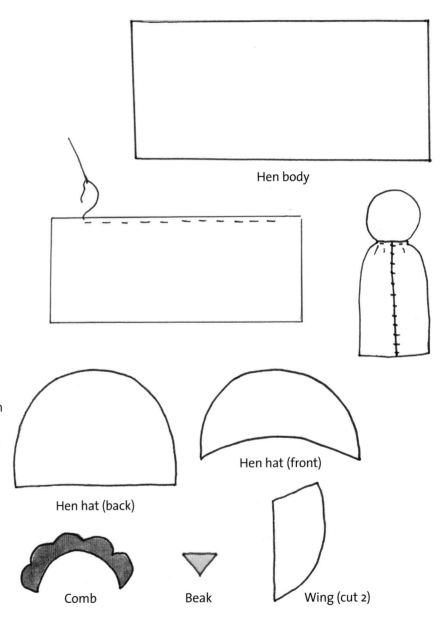

Hen body

Hen hat (back)

Hen hat (front)

Comb

Beak

Wing (cut 2)

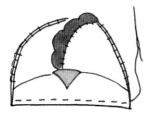

7. Starting 5 mm (¼ in) up from the front-center edge of the hat, use red embroidery floss to stitch the red scalloped comb from front to back along the top-center of the hat.

8. With two strands of matching embroidery floss, sew a running stitch along the bottom edge of the back of the hat and gather slightly to fit the contour of the doll's head.

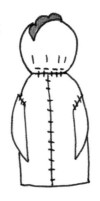

9. Glue the hat onto the doll and add the yellow beak piece to the front of the hat beneath the start of the comb.

10. If you wish, add a few stitches to join the back of the hat to the back of the felt body piece.

Adding wings

11. Cut two wings from felt according to the pattern and glue or sew to the sides of the body.

BABY CHICKS

Wing (cut 2)

Painting the doll

1. Using 3 cm (1³⁄₁₆ in) tot-pegs, paint the bodies pale yellow, leaving circular space for painting the faces.

2. Paint faces on the dolls.

Adding wings

3. Cut wings from pale yellow felt and glue them to the sides of the bodies.

Chapter Two

Summer

Mermaids

I had a lot of fun designing these mermaids and created many variations. I experimented creating mermaids with green and blue glittered tails, mermaids with elegant seaweed cloche-chapeaux, mermaids with flowing hair and yet more mermaids with sea-sprite antennae. I wonder what mermaid designs you will dream up...

SUPPLIES

5 cm (2 in) angel-pegs

4 cm (1⅝ in) boy-pegs

Wool felt: Green and/or blue

Paper flower stamens (or thin-gauge wire and beads)

Tiny seashells

Matching embroidery floss and needles

Watercolor paint and brushes

Fabric scissors

Tracing paper or a photocopy of patterns

A pencil

Glue

Who would be
A mermaid fair,
Singing alone,
Combing her hair
Under the sea,
In a golden curl
With a comb of pearl,
On a throne?

I would be a mermaid fair;
I would sing to myself the whole of the day;
With a comb of pearl I would comb my hair;
And still as I comb'd I would sing and say,
'Who is it loves me? Who loves not me?'
I would comb my hair till my ringlets would fall
Low adown, low adown,
From under my starry sea-bud crown...

Alfred Tennyson

Painting the dolls

1. Paint a face and hair on a 5 cm (2 in) angel-peg for the larger mermaid or a 4 cm (1⅝ in) boy-peg for a smaller mermaid.

2. With a pencil, lightly draw a line around the middle of the doll body to distinguish the upper torso from tail, and then, using two contrasting colors (I used blues and greens), paint the torso in one color and the tail in another color.

3. When the paint on the lower tail portion is dry, you can add tiny fish-scales, or, if you wish, paint on a layer of diluted glue and add some glitter.

Making the hat

4. To make the mermaid hat, cut out wool felt according to the pattern. Overlap the two straight sides, adjust to fit the head of the doll and, using a flat appliqué fell-stitch, sew to form a cone shape. Then tack the point of the cone down at the back to form a bonnet.

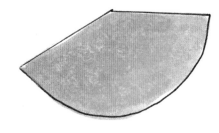

Hat

5. If you'd like to add antennae, make a tiny snip with sharp scissors at each corner of the bonnet on the right and left, and then slip the ends of the antennae inside. I used paper flower stamens which are available for making artificial flowers. If you cannot find paper flower stamens, you can make your own antennae by looping a small bead on the end of a bit of fine-gauge wire.

6. Put a small amount of glue inside the hat and place on the head of the doll (after the hat is glued, you can adjust the height of the antennae) and finally, for a bit of panache, you can decorate the hat with a tiny seashell.

Adding the tail

7. To add the tail, cut out a tail pattern-piece and glue to the back of the doll.

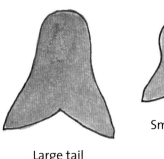

Large tail

Small tail

Dandelions

There is a magic to the childhood ritual of making a wish then blowing on a dandelion to watch the seeds of this wish fly to the wind. Even now, when I see a dandelion flower or a flurry of tiny seeds float by, I think of my own childhood hopes and also the whispered wishes of my children as I teach them this sweet ritual anew.

SUPPLIES

5 cm (2 in) angel-pegs

4 cm (1⅝ in) boy-pegs

Wool felt: green

White, fuzzy, lace-weight yarn (a silk-mohair blend is ideal)

2.75 mm (size 1) crochet hook

Watercolor paint and brushes

Tracing paper or a photocopy of patterns for leaves

Fabric scissors

A pencil

Glue

Little Dandelion

Bright little Dandelion

Lights up the meads,

Swings on her slender foot,

Telleth her beads,

Lists to the robin's note

Poured from above;

Wise little Dandelion

Asks not for love.

Pale little Dandelion,

In her white shroud,

Heareth the angel-breeze

Call from the cloud;

Tiny plumes fluttering

Make no delay;

Little winged Dandelion

Soareth away.

Helen Barron Bostwick

Painting the dolls

1. Paint a white cap and face on a 5 cm (2 in) angel-peg for a larger dandelion or a 4 cm (1⁵⁄₈ in) boy-peg for a smaller dandelion.

2. Paint the body of the doll a pale green.

3. When the paint on the body is dry, paint a calyx-collar around the neck.

Crocheting the dandelion cap

Using white lace-weight yarn (silk-mohair blend) and a 2.75 mm (size 1) crochet hook:

Beg Rnd: Chain 3-4 stitches, slip stitch into first single crochet (sc) to join into a ring.
Rnd 1: Sc 12 into ring. Place marker in first stitch of every round to keep track of the rounds.

Rnd 2: *sc twice in first stitch (i.e. increase), sc in next 2 stitches,* repeat 6 times (you will end up with 16 sc).
Rnd 3-6: Sc 16 around.

Check sizing of hat on the peg doll. If you crochet loosely, the hat may already fit, and if it does, you can fasten off and weave in ends. If the hat is too small, proceed to Rnd 7.

Rnd 7: *sc 7, dec 1,* repeat 2 times. Check the fit of the hat again. If it fits, fasten off and weave in ends. If the hat is still too small, sc 7 or 8 (halfway through the round) and check sizing again.

When the hat fits the doll (and you have secured the ends of your yarn), apply a bit of glue to the head and arrange the hat in place. When the glue is dry, you can use your fingers to gently pull fibers loose to create a fuzzy look for the cap.

Adding leaves

4. Cut out leaves from green felt according to the pattern and glue onto the body of your doll.

Harvest from the Garden

This year in my garden, I'm growing carrots, cabbages, corn, tomatoes, radishes and peas. What vegetables are you growing in your garden? Perhaps you have a few fruit trees or a nearby Farmer's Market where you can gather tiny sweet cherries, strawberries, peaches, plums and apples too...

SUPPLIES

6 cm (2⅜ in) standard wood-people-pegs

4 cm (1⅝ in) boy-pegs

3 cm (1³⁄₁₆ in) baby/bee pegs

Watercolor paint and brushes

Wool felt: red, light and dark green, light and dark yellow

Thin-gauge, white fabric-wrapped floral wire

Matching embroidery floss and needles

A small amount of wool stuffing

Tracing paper or a photocopy of patterns

Beeswax polish (optional)

Fabric scissors

A pencil

Glue

The country vegetables scorn
To lie about in shops,
They stand upright as they were born
In neatly-patterned crops;

And when you want your dinner you
Don't buy it from a shelf,
You find a lettuce fresh with dew
And pull it for yourself;

You pick an apronful of peas
And shell them on the spot.
You cut a cabbage, if you please,
To pop into the pot.

The folks who their potatoes buy
From sacks before they sup,
Miss half of the potato's joy,
And that's to dig it up.

Eleanor Farjeon

CARROT

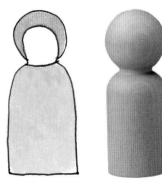

Painting the doll

1. Using a 6 cm (2⅜ in) standard wood-people-peg, paint the head a bright orange (leaving an unpainted oval for the face) and the body a pale green.

2. Paint a collar of leaves on the body of the doll (around the neck).

3. Paint a face inside the unpainted oval.

Making the hat

4. Cut the front and back pieces of the carrot hat from bright orange felt according to the pattern. Then, using a blanket stitch, sew around the sides and top.

5. Add embroidery details if you wish. You can also add a small root to the very top. I made the end of the carrot root using white floral wire which I painted orange to match the felt. It's inserted between the stitches at the top of the hat and secured with a bit of glue inside.

6. With two strands of matching embroidery floss, sew a running stitch along the bottom edge of the back of the hat and gather slightly to fit the contour of the doll's head.

7. Loosely fill the inside of the hat with a bit of wool stuffing and glue onto the head of the doll.

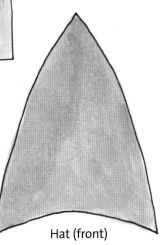

Hat (front)

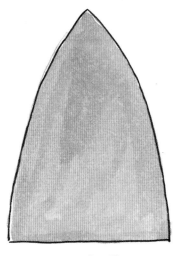

Hat (back)

CORN

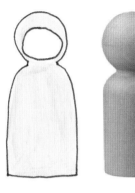

Painting the doll

1. Using a 6 cm (2⅜ in) standard wood-people-peg, paint the head and body a pale yellow color, leaving an unpainted oval for the face.

2. Paint a face inside the unpainted oval.

Corn kernel

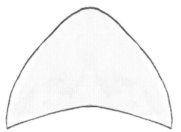

Hat (front)

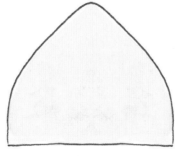

Hat (back)

Making the hat

3. Cut out front and back hat pieces from pale yellow felt, plus approximately 20 corn kernels from a brighter yellow felt. Using a blanket stitch, sew the hat pieces together and add a few strands of pale yellow embroidery floss at the top to form the corn-silk tassel. This is done by stitching some large loops from the top of the hat, securing them around their base with a few stitches and then snipping the loops at the top.

4. With two strands of matching embroidery floss, sew a running stitch along the bottom edge of the back of the hat and gather slightly to fit the contour of the doll's head.

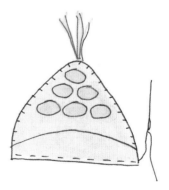

5. Loosely fill the inside of the hat with wool stuffing, glue the hat onto the head of the doll, and then glue bright yellow felt kernel pieces into place on the front of the hat and down the front of the doll's body.

CABBAGE

Painting the doll

1. Using a 6 cm (2⅜ in) standard wood-people-peg, paint the head and body a medium green color, leaving an unpainted oval for the face. Use a beeswax rub for a richer tone and light sheen (optional).

2. Paint a face inside the unpainted oval.

Adding leaves

3. Using the cabbage leaf pattern, cut two leaves from a lighter green felt and nine leaves from a darker green. Glue the two lighter leaves in front, below the face of the doll, and layer the rest of the leaves around the body.

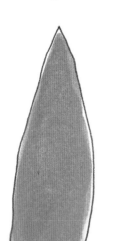

Leaf (cut 3–4)

Adding leaves

6. Cut out three or four leaves according to the leaf pattern and glue around the sides and back of the doll.

Leaf

TOMATO

Painting the doll

1. Using a 6 cm (2⅜ in) standard wood-people-peg, paint the head and body a bright red color, leaving an unpainted oval for the face. Use a beeswax rub for a richer tone and light sheen (optional).

Making the hat

3. Cut out front and back hat pieces from bright red felt, plus the stem calyx from dark green felt and, using a blanket stitch, sew around the top of the hat.

4. With 2 strands of matching embroidery floss, sew a running stitch along the bottom edge of the back of the hat and gather slightly to fit the contour of the doll's head.

2. Paint a face inside the unpainted oval.

Calyx

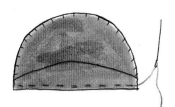

5. Glue the hat onto the head of the doll and the calyx onto the top of the hat.

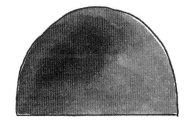

Hat (back)

Hat (front)

RADISH

Painting the doll

1. Using a 4 cm (1⅝ in) boy-peg, paint the head a bright red (leaving an unpainted oval for the face) and the body a pale green.

2. Paint a collar of leaves on the body of the doll (around the neck).

3. Paint a face inside the unpainted oval.

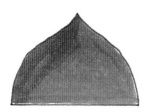

Hat (back)　　　　　Hat (front)

Making the hat

4. According to the pattern of the radish hat, cut the front and back pieces from red felt. Then, using a blanket stitch, sew around the top and sides of the hat.

5. You can also add a small root to the very top. I made the end of the radish root using white floral wire which I painted red to match the felt. It's inserted between the stitches at the top of the hat and secured with a bit of glue inside.

6. With two strands of matching embroidery floss, sew a running stitch along the bottom edge of the back of the hat and gather slightly to fit the contour of the doll's head.

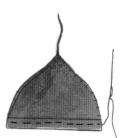

7. Glue the hat onto the head of the doll.

PEAS IN A POD

Painting the dolls

1. Using 3 cm (1³/₁₆ in) bee-shape pegs, paint the heads and bodies a bright medium green, leaving unpainted circles for the faces. For a deeper tone, rub painted areas with beeswax polish (optional).

2. Paint faces on the dolls.

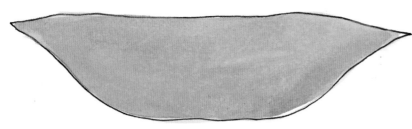

Pod (cut 2)

Making the pod

3. Cut out two pieces of green felt according to the peapod pattern. Using a blanket stitch, sew around the bottom edges and approximately 2 cm (³/₄ in) on either end of the top of the pod (this should leave a sufficient opening in the center to hold the dolls).

Bees, Butterflies and Ladybirds

SUPPLIES

5 cm (2 in) angel-pegs

3 cm (1³/₁₆ in) tot-pegs

Watercolor paint (plus gold and black acrylic paints) plus brushes

Wool felt: blues, pinks, yellow, black and red

Thin-gauge, fabric-wrapped floral wire

Matching embroidery floss and needles

Paper flower stamens (or thin-gauge wire and beads)

Yellow wool roving, a notched felting needle and a thick foam block

Tracing paper or a photocopy of patterns

Fabric scissors and pinking shears

A pencil

Glue

BUTTERFLY

Painting the doll

1. Using a 5 cm (2 in) angel-peg cover the head and body with brown paint, leaving an unpainted circle for the face.

Making the hat

4. Cut out front and back pieces of the butterfly hat according to the pattern and sew around the top using a blanket stitch. To add antennae, use the tip of a knitting needle to enlarge the space between two stitches and then insert antennae. I made antennae from paper flower stamens which are available for making artificial flowers. If you cannot find paper flower stamens, you can make your own antennae by looping a small bead on the end of a bit of fine-gauge, fabric-wrapped floral wire.

2. When the paint is dry you can add any ornamentation you wish to the body; I painted a series of gold dots.

Hat (front)

Hat (back)

5. With two strands of matching embroidery floss, sew a running stitch along the bottom edge of the back of the hat and gather slightly to fit the contour of the doll's head.

3. Paint a face on your doll.

6. Put a small amount of glue inside the hat and glue onto the head of the doll.

Adding wings

7. Cut out wings according to the patterns and glue onto the back of the doll.

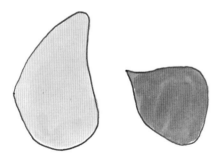

WIngs (cut 2 of each piece)

BEE

Painting the doll

1. Using a 3 cm (1³⁄₁₆ in) tot-peg, paint the head and body yellow, leaving a small unpainted oval or circle for the face.

2. Paint a face on your doll and add any other painted embellishments you wish (I added a tiny golden button on the chest).

Wing

Body stripes (cut 2 black and 1 yellow)

Decorating the doll's body

3. Cut 3 strips of felt, 2 of black, 5 mm (³⁄₁₆ in) wide by 5.5 cm (2¹⁄₈ in) and one of yellow 7 mm (¼ in). I needle felted a little bit of yellow roving onto the yellow felt to add dimension and give it a fuzzy look.

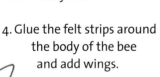

4. Glue the felt strips around the body of the bee and add wings.

Adding antennae

5. Using pinking shears, cut a thin strip 4 cm (1½ in) long from black felt. Apply glue and wrap around the head. To attach antennae, slip the ends of the antennae (made from paper flower stamens or thin-gauge, fabric-wrapped floral wire) into the glued area between the doll's head and the felt crown.

Crown

LADYBIRD

Wing

Painting the doll

1. Using a 3 cm (1³/₁₆ in) tot-peg, paint the body and head black, leaving a small circle or oval for the face.

Adding wings

4. To make the ladybird wings, cut them from red felt according to the pattern. I needle felted black dots onto my ladybird wings; however, sewing or gluing tiny black dots cut from felt would work equally well, as would embroidering dots with a bit of embroidery floss. After you have added black dots, glue the wings to the back of your ladybird.

2. Paint a face on your doll and add any other painted embellishments you wish (I added a tiny golden button on the chest).

Adding antennae

3. With pinking shears, cut a thin strip 4 cm (1½ in) long from black felt. Apply glue and wrap around the head. Paint a pair of antennae (made from paper flower stamens or thin-gauge, fabric-wrapped floral wire) with black acrylic paint. To attach them, slip the ends into the glued area between the doll's head and the felt crown.

Crown

Summer Garden Sprites

SUPPLIES

4 cm (1⅝ in) boy-pegs

Wool felt in a variety of colors

Matching embroidery floss and needles

Watercolor paint and brushes

Paper flower stamens (or thin-gauge wire and beads)

Tracing paper or a photocopy of patterns

Fabric scissors and pinking shears

Beeswax polish (optional)

A ruler

A pencil

Glue

The little shoes that fairies wear
Are very small indeed;
No larger than a violet bud,
As tiny as a seed.

The little shoes of fairies are
So light and soft and small
That though a million passed you by
You would not hear at all.

Annette Wynne

Painting the dolls

1. Using 4 cm (1⅝ in) boy-pegs, paint hair and a face on each.

Making the hats

3. Cut hats for your sprites from felt in colors which suit your summer garden fancies. Overlap the two straight sides, adjust to fit the heads of the dolls. Using a flat appliqué fell-stitch, sew to form cone shapes and glue onto the heads of your dolls.

2. Paint the bodies of your sprites to match the colors of summer garden flowers and (optional) rub with a beeswax polish.

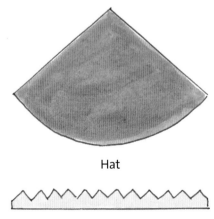

Hat

Crown

4. To decorate the hats, use pinking shears to cut 6.5 cm (2½ in) lengths of felt in contrasting colors. Secure the ornamental sections around the bases of the hats with glue, and then insert antennae into the glue between the two sections of the hat. You can make antennae from paper flower stamens or short lengths of fabric-wrapped floral wire with beads looped on the ends.

Adding wings

5. According to the pattern, cut wings from contrasting colors of felt and glue onto the backs of your dolls.

Wings

Making flowers

6. Cut out the desired flower shape from felt and snip the line between A and B as indicated on the pattern.

7. Overlap A and B, and, to add the stem, sandwich a piece of fabric-wrapped floral wire between the layers of A and B when you glue them together. (Note: the long end of the floral wire should come through the center of the flower – not through the end of the petal).

8. Add beads or other decoration (such as a bit of glitter) to the center of your flower according to your preference.

Flowers

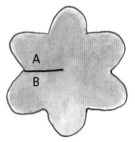

Chapter Three

Autumn

Toadstool Gnomes

… It led me with remembered things

Into an old-time vale,

Peopled with faery glimmerings,

And flower-like fancies pale;

Where fungus forms stood, gold and gray,

Each in its mushroom gown,

And, roofed with red, glimpsed far away,

A little toadstool town.

Madison Cawein

SUPPLIES

5 cm (2 in) angel-peg

4 cm (1⅝ in) boy-pegs

3 cm (1³⁄₁₆ in) tot-peg

Watercolor paint (plus opaque red acrylic paint) and brushes

A pencil

Toadstool

To create your own little toadstool from a plain wooden cupboard knob:

1. Paint the top red and the bottom white.

2. Add white specks to the top. You're done!

Painting the dolls

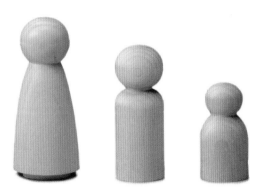

1. Paint hair and faces on a 5 cm (2 in) angel-peg for the toadstool-gnome mama, 4 cm (1⅝ in) boy-pegs for the children and a 3 cm (1³⁄₁₆ in) tot-peg for the baby. I also used a pencil to draw eyeglasses on my mama-gnome!

2. Using opaque acrylic paint for the caps (or thick watercolor paint diluted with very little water), paint red caps over the heads. Once the red paint is thoroughly dry, use an opaque white acrylic paint to add dots to the caps.

3. For autumn toadstool-gnomes blend white paint downwards, fading into a light brown to cover the bodies of the dolls. I also painted some tiny buttons.

4. For springtime toadstool-gnomes, paint the bodies white and add blades of bright green grass around the base of each doll.

Acorn Gnomes

'Oh I'll never be big,' the acorn said
As it gazed on high to the oak tree tall,
'I'm little and round as a miller's thumb,
I'll never be big, I'll always be small.'

The oak tree smiled a knowing smile,
'My trunk is thick, and my roots are deep,
My branches and twigs spread high and wide,
For birds to nest in, and bugs to sleep.

But I was an acorn too on a time,
"Oh I'll never be big, I'll never be strong,"
That's what I thought many years ago...
And, dear little acorn, you see I was wrong!'

Paul King

SUPPLIES
4 cm (1⅝ in) boy-size pegs
Acorn caps to fit the heads of your dolls
Watercolor paints and brushes
Glue

These are the most basic of all peg dolls to create and are perfect for display on an Autumn Nature Table.

Acorns

1. In the autumn gather acorn caps and match them to fit the heads of your dolls. The acorn caps I found fit the heads of the 4 cm (1⅝ in) boy-size pegs.
2. Glue the acorn caps onto the heads of your dolls.

Painting the dolls

3. Paint faces on your dolls.

4. Paint the bodies of your dolls in autumnal colors. When the paint is dry, rub with beeswax polish (optional).

Gnome Family and their Toadstool Home

SUPPLIES

Two 5 cm (2 in) angel-pegs
Two 4 cm (1⅝ in) boy-pegs
One 3 cm (1³⁄₁₆ in) tot-peg
Watercolor paint and brushes
Wool felt: red, tan and brown
Wide ribbon, approximately 122 cm (48 in)
A bit of brown yarn
A notched felting-needle and thick foam block
Wool roving: white and brown (or grey)
Matching embroidery floss and needles
Tracing paper or a photocopy of patterns
Beeswax polish (optional)
Fabric scissors
A pencil
Glue

Once there was a large field with flowers and grasses and one mushroom growing on it. Under the mushroom lived Mr. and Mrs. Troll and their children. They had lived there for quite some time. The children played happily among the tall flowers and grasses. Mrs. Troll fussed with her pots and pans and was content. 'What a pleasant, peaceful way we live,' said Mrs. Troll...

From *Under a Mushroom* by Anita Lobel

In the course of Anita Lobel's wonderful story *Under a Mushroom,* it begins to rain and the little family welcomes an assortment of fanciful creatures beneath their mushroom to shelter from the storm.

Inspired by this tale, I've made a tiny family of dolls who live beneath a mushroom. My dolls are not trolls, but gnomes... Still, I wonder whether there might be room under their mushroom, too, for a little Glump? A Schnooze? A Dimle? Perhaps a Gizzygonk and a Dizzydonk, or maybe a group of Gleeps?

Painting the dolls

Painting the dolls

1. Paint hair and faces on 5 cm (2 in) angel-pegs for the mama and papa gnomes, 4 cm (1⅝ in) boy-pegs for the children and a 3 cm (1³⁄₁₆ in) tot-peg for the baby.

2. Paint the bodies and add embellishments (for the papa-gnome I painted a fine, black belt and everyone else received shiny gold buttons). Rub the bodies with a beeswax polish (optional).

Hat for papa, mama and child gnome

Hat for baby gnome

Making the hats

3. Cut out hats according to the patterns. Then overlap the two straight sides, adjust to fit the head of the doll and, using a flat appliqué fell-stitch, sew to form a cone shape. Glue onto the heads of the dolls. If you would like to add plaits to your mama-gnome, prepare them from brown yarn and glue them beneath her hat.

Adding a beard to Papa Gnome

4. To create a beard for your papa-gnome, take a few wisps of wool and fold the fibers in half. Place your fibers on a piece of thick foam, give them a few stabs across the folded area with your felting-needle and then, with the tip of your needle, start pulling in bits of fiber from the sides and over the top. Keep stabbing and pulling in bits of fiber until you have a more densely felted area at the top and wisps of unfelted beard hanging down. Finally, trim your beard across the top (if necessary) and sides to neaten things up. You can also trim and shape the beard along the bottom edge, if you wish. When you are satisfied with the shape of the beard, glue it onto the lower portion of the face of your doll.

Alternatively, if you don't want to needle-felt a beard, you could use a few wisps of unfelted roving or bits of yarn to create a beard for your doll. And yet another way to make a beard would be to cut a small piece of brown or grey felt into shape and glue it on the face of your doll.

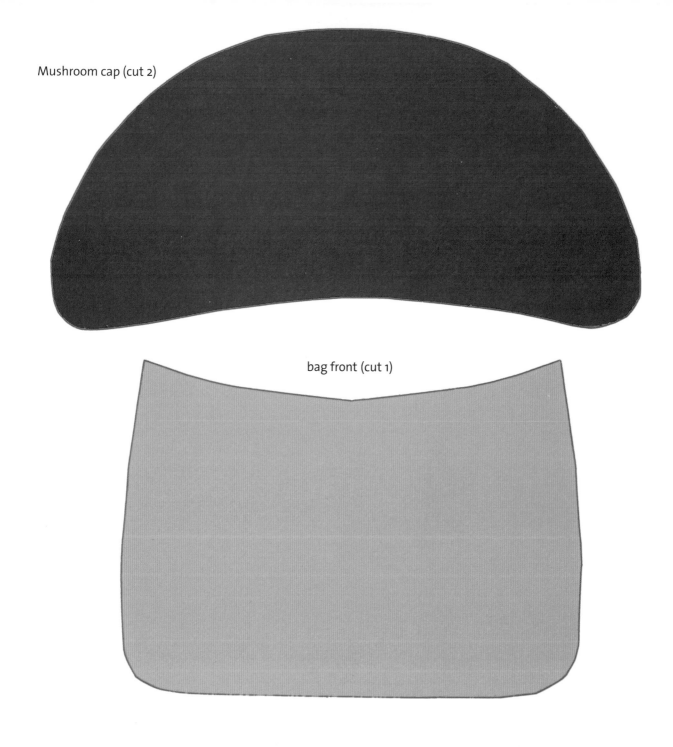

Mushroom cap (cut 2)

bag front (cut 1)

TOADSTOOL BAG INSTRUCTIONS

Cutting out pattern pieces

1. Cut out all pieces according to the patterns – one bag-front piece from light beige felt, two bag-backing pieces (I cut them from brown felt) and two red mushroom-cap pieces.

bag back (cut 2)

Sewing

2. Place the two back pieces together and then the shorter front piece on top; pin in place so the bottom edges of all three pieces are aligned. Using a blanket stitch, sew around the sides and bottom of the pieces; you can also finish the top edge of the shorter front piece with a blanket stitch to reinforce it.

Adding white dots

3. To needle-felt the white dots onto the red cap of the toadstool, place one of your red toadstool cap pieces onto a very thick piece of dense foam, then take a tiny wisp of white wool roving and roll it into a loose ball between your fingers. Place the tiny ball of wool onto the red mushroom-cap piece and stab repeatedly with a notched felting needle. When you are satisfied that the first wool dot is securely in place, add several more dots scattered around the mushroom cap until you are happy with how your mushroom cap looks.

If you don't want to use a needle-felting technique, you could appliqué white dots cut from wool felt for similar results.

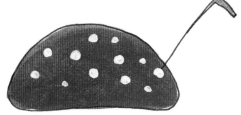

Assembling the toadstool cap

4. Cover the back of your dotted toadstool-cap with the second piece of red felt and pin the two pieces together. Then pin the curved top of your mushroom cap to the top edge of the bag. Using a blanket stitch, sew around the edges of the mushroom cap, and as you come over the curved top you will also sew the top of the red cap to the back section of the bag.

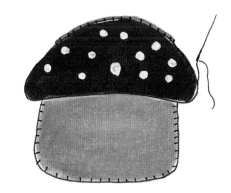

Adding a shoulder strap

5. Pin the ends of a length of ribbon, approximately 122 cm (48 in), onto the back of the bag and stitch in place.

Owls

I loosely based the design of these owls on a drawing I found of a great horned owl -- the very same type of owl who sits in the pine trees at the top of my garden hooting softly at 3 a.m. Please feel free to adapt the design to match any of your own local, resident owls!

A wise old owl sat in an oak.

The more he heard, the less he spoke,

The less he spoke, the more he heard.

How I wish to be like that wise old bird...

Anonymous

SUPPLIES

6 cm (2⅜ in) standard wood-people-pegs

Watercolor paint and brushes

Wool felt: brown and golden-yellow

Brown wool roving, a notched felting-needle and thick foam block

Matching embroidery floss and needles

Tracing paper or a photocopy of patterns

Fabric scissors

A pencil

Glue

Painting the dolls

1. Using a 6 cm (2³⁄₈ in) standard wood-people-peg, paint the body and head brown, leaving the chest and stomach unpainted, plus an unpainted oval for the face.

2. Add a face to the doll.

3. Paint the stomach and chest grey, add an arc of ochre-colored paint around the grey area and blend the edges of the ochre and grey together. When the grey and ochre painted section is dry, add tiny black feather details on the stomach and chest area of the doll.

Making the hat

4. From brown wool felt, cut out and align the front and back hat pieces along the curve of the top of the hat. Then, using two strands of matching embroidery floss, sew around the top.

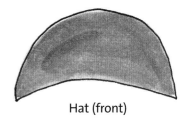

Hat (front)

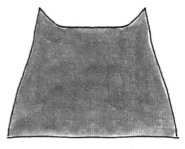

Hat (back)

5. To create the ear-tufts, take a tiny wisp of brown wool roving to match your hat color and fold the fibers of the roving in half and half again. Then place the hat on a thick piece

of dense foam and place your little fiber bundle on one of the pointed ears. With your felting needle, start stabbing one end of your little fiber-bundle through the felt of one of the little points on top of the hat. Between stabs, use your needle to pull straying wisps of fiber in towards the felt point where you are securing your fibers. When you are satisfied that your fibers are secured, use a sharp scissor to trim the fibers at the sides and across the top of the wispy little ear-tuft you've created for your owl. Then repeat the process for the other ear-tuft.

Alternately, if you don't have needle-felting materials on hand, you could stitch fuzzy bits of yarn in place, add a bit of feather or leave the ear-tufts plain (the little peaks at the sides of the hat are terribly cute, all on their own and unadorned!)

Adding wings

8. Cut out the wings and glue them to the sides of the doll.

6. With two strands of matching brown embroidery floss, sew a running stitch along the bottom edge of the back of the hat and gather slightly to fit the contour of the doll's head.

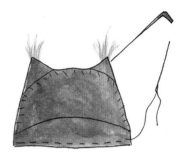

Beak

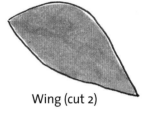

Wing (cut 2)

7. Glue the hat onto the doll and add the yellow beak piece to the front of the hat at the center.

Michaelmas

'What's your mind always occupied about?' asked the Boy. 'That's what I want to know.' The dragon coloured slightly and looked away. Presently he said bashfully: 'Did you ever—just for fun—try to make up poetry— verses, you know?'

From *The Reluctant Dragon* by Kenneth Grahame

SUPPLIES

Two 6 cm (2⅜ in) standard wood-people-pegs

A 4 cm (1⅝ in) boy-peg

Watercolor paint and brushes

Wool felt: grey, blue, light and dark green, golden-yellow and reddish-orange

Matching embroidery floss and needles

Tracing paper or a photocopy of patterns

Beeswax polish (optional)

Fabric scissors

A pencil

Glue

Michaelmas is a Christian festival observed on September 29th, and as part of the Michaelmas celebration, it is a tradition to tell the story of St. George and the Dragon. I always love a good story, however I find the legend of St. George and the Dragon somewhat unsettling because I know that, at the end of the story, the dragon will be destroyed. I am comforted only in small measure to know that no actual dragons were harmed in the fabrication of this story because originally, the dragon was a metaphor for those who resisted the fighters of the Crusades. Still, I much prefer the story of *The Reluctant Dragon* by Kenneth Grahame. In this story the dragon is a gentle, misunderstood beast who writes poetry and makes purring noises when he is feeling content. The dragon befriends a little boy, and when St. George comes to town looking for a fight, the child convinces St. George that there is no need to battle the rather naive creature. There are still complications to work out; in this peaceful story, unfounded prejudice and fear of the unknown must be overcome. And as for the end of the tale, I will leave you to curl up with a child or two and discover it for yourselves.

I have created these versions of St. George and the Dragon so that you can re-enact your own version of the story. To my own tableau I have added the figure of a little boy to serve as conqueror over the scourge of unfounded bias and discrimination.

ST GEORGE

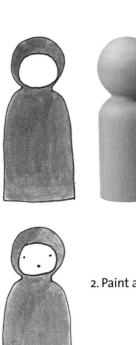

Painting the doll

1. Using a 6 cm (2⅜ in) standard wood-people-peg, paint the body and head grey, leaving an unpainted oval for the face.

2. Paint a face on your doll.

Feather

Chest plate

Face grille

Helmet (back)

Helmet (front)

The helmet

3. Cut all three pieces for the helmet from grey wool felt according to the pattern. Align the curved tops of the front and back pieces and, using a blanket stitch, sew around the top. Then fold the helmet from side to side (across the seam) and add a running stitch from the top-center down the front (this will form a small ridge down the front of the helmet).

4. Cut three tiny strips of blue felt and glue them to the face-grille portion of the helmet, and while the glue is drying you can tack the feather to the top of the helmet.

5. Sew a running-stitch across the bottom of the back of the helmet and gather slightly so that the helmet will fit the contour of the doll's head.

6. Tack the face-grille at the sides of the helmet so that it will cover the lower portion of the doll's face and glue helmet onto the head of the doll.

The chest plate

7. Cut out the chest-plate from blue wool felt and glue to the doll's chest.

THE DRAGON

Painting the doll

1. Using a 6 cm (2⅜ in) standard wood-people-peg, paint the body and head green, leaving an unpainted oval for the face. For a deeper tone and a soft sheen, polish with a beeswax rub (optional).

2. Paint a face on your doll. For a slightly fierce look (which may belie the dragon's true, gentle nature) I used a pencil to add some eyebrows.

Making the headdress

3. Cut all pieces for the dragon's headdress from green wool felt according to the patterns. All pieces will be in a lighter green to match the body of the dragon except for the piece which will form the spine ridges of the dragon. That piece should be cut from a darker, contrasting green.

4. Align the top curves of the front and back pieces of the headdress. Using a blanket stitch, sew the two pieces together over the top curve.

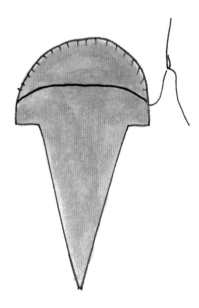

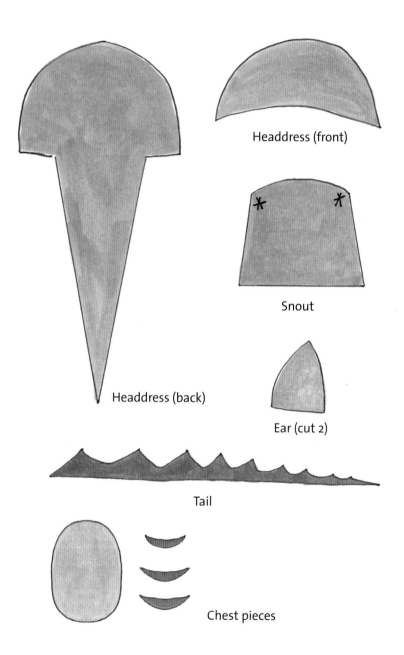

Headdress (front)

Snout

Headdress (back)

Ear (cut 2)

Tail

Chest pieces

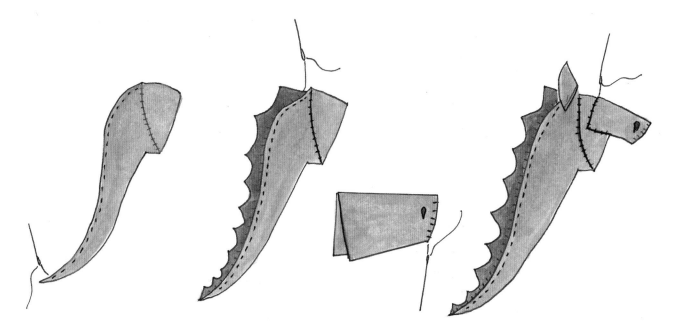

5. Then, fold the long back piece lengthwise and add a running stitch from the top of the headdress down to the tip of the tail, to form a small ridge. With small stitches, tack the dark green spine along the raised ridge down the back of the dragon's headdress.

6. Fold the snout-piece so that the stars on the pattern are aligned and, using a blanket stitch, sew along the front, curved portion. Add touches of embroidery to indicate the dragon's nostrils, then position this snout piece over the front of the headdress so the snout protrudes but does not cover the face. Sew the snout piece in place.

7. Tack the ears to the sides of the headdress and glue the headdress in place (note: you will glue it onto the head and half-way down the back of the doll. See photos of the doll on pages 108 and 115 for guidance).

The chestplate

8. Cut the chest-plate for the dragon from wool felt and a few small strips of a contrasting color for chest-plate details. Glue the chest-plate to the front of the dragon and then glue the contrasting strips of felt on top of this.

THE BOY

Painting the doll

1. Paint hair and a face on a 4 cm (1⅝ in) boy-peg.

2. Paint the body of the doll, and for a soft sheen, polish with a beeswax rub (optional).

Martinmas

Martinmas, celebrated on November 11th, is a harvest feast which commemorates the compassionate spirit of St. Martin, who, as legend tells, gave away half his cloak to warm a shivering pauper. For children, the festival is traditionally celebrated by constructing small lanterns and walking with them in procession accompanied by song. The symbolism of this lantern procession during the darkening days of autumn is very beautiful. The authors of *All Year Round* (Druitt, Fynes-Clinton, Rowling; Hawthorn Press) describe it thus:

When we make a paper lantern, we may feel we are giving protection to our own little 'flame'... so that we may carry it safely through the dark world. It may only be a small and fragile light – but every light brings relief to the darkness.

> The sunlight fast is dwindling,
> My little lamp needs kindling,
> It's beam shines far in darkest night,
> Dear lantern guard me with your light.

'Song' Anonymous.
From *Festivals, Family and Food*, Hawthorn Press.

SUPPLIES

6 cm (2⅜ in) standard wood-people-pegs

Watercolor paint and brushes

Wool felt: cream-colored, plus a selection of autumnal colors

Double-pointed 4 mm (US 6) needles

dk/worsted yarn in autumnal colors

Thin-gauge wire (preferably fabric-wrapped floral wire)

Matching embroidery floss and needles

Tracing paper or a photocopy of patterns

A small amount of wool stuffing

Beeswax polish (optional)

Fabric scissors

A ruler

A pencil

Glue

DOLLS

Painting the doll

1. Paint hair and a face on a 6 cm (2⅜ in) standard wood-people-peg.

2. Choose an autumnal color and paint the body of the doll. For a soft sheen, polish with a beeswax rub (optional).

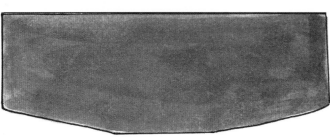

Cloak

Cloaks

3. Cut small strips of dark-colored felt, approximately 2½ cm (1 in) by 1 cm (⅜ in) and glue the ends of the strip to the sides of the dolls so that there is a small, raised loop of felt in the center (this will hold the lantern poles beneath the cloak).

Lantern pocket

4. From wool felt, cut cloaks for the dolls according to the pattern. Sew a running-stitch across the top of each cloak, gather slightly to fit around the necks of the dolls and knot thread. To hold the cloaks in place, put a bit of glue around the shoulders of each doll and secure the top of the cloaks at the front with a stitch or two of embroidery floss. When the glue is dry, press the side of the cloak gently with your fingers and find the raised loop of felt glued to the side of the doll. Using sharp scissors, make a small horizontal cut in each cloak just above the loop of felt. This will enable you to slip a lantern pole through the cloak and into the felt loop which will hold the pole in place.

Knitting the hats

5. These dolls would look charming in any sort of hat (or even with no hats at all); however, given the fact that they are making an autumn evening procession, I thought that knit caps might be a nice way to keep their tiny noggins warm.

INSTRUCTIONS
Using dk/worsted yarn with 4 mm (US 6) needles:
Cast on (CO) 14 stitches, join to work in the round.

Rows 1-2: knit all stitches (14)

Row 3: k2, *k2tog, k2* repeat between the *'s to the end of the row (11)

Row 4: knit (11)

Row 5: (k2tog, k2) twice, k2tog, k1 (8)

Row 6: *k2tog, k2* repeat between the *'s to the end of the row (6)

Row 7: k2tog around (3)

Cut yarn, pull through remaining stitches, secure inside hat.

Lanterns

Lantern (cut 4)

6. From pale cream-colored felt, cut four lantern pieces according to the pattern. Sew the sides of the pieces together so that the tips form a point at the bottom and there is an open space at the top. Place a tiny bit of wool stuffing inside the lantern to help it hold its shape.

7. Sew loops of thread over the top for hanging the lantern.

8. To form the poles, any type of thin, flexible wire will do. I used two lengths of thin, fabric-wrapped floral wire 10 cm (4 in), twisted them together, shaped them into a crook and added a hook at the end to hold the lantern. If the end of your pole slides out of the little pocket glued to the side of the doll (under the cloak), you can try wrapping it with a bit of sticky-tape or paper to keep it more firmly in place inside the pocket. It is nice, however, to be able to remove the lanterns from the dolls. The lanterns are a bit fragile and not suitable if young children wish to play with the dolls.

Halloween

SUPPLIES

6 cm (2³⁄₈ in) standard people-pegs

4 cm (1⁵⁄₈ in) boy-pegs

Watercolor paint and brushes

Wool felt: black, white and grey

Matching embroidery floss and needles

Tracing paper or a photocopy of patterns

Beeswax polish (optional)

Chenille wire (wire pipe-cleaner)

Fabric scissors

A pencil

A ruler

Glue

There was an old woman toss'd up in a basket,

Seventeen times as high as the moon;

Where she was going I couldn't but ask it,

For in her hand she carried a broom.

'Old woman, old woman, old woman,' quoth I,

'O whither, O whither, O whither so high?'

'To brush the cobwebs off the sky!'

'May I go with you?'

'Aye, by-and-by.'

Traditional

WITCH

Painting the doll

1. Paint hair and a face on a 6 cm (2⅜ in) standard people-peg for the larger witch or a 4 cm (1⅝ in) boy-peg for a smaller witch.

2. Paint the body of the doll black and (optional) rub with beeswax polish.

Making the hat

3. From black wool felt, cut out the two pieces for the witch's hat (note: there are two sets of pattern pieces; one set for the larger doll and one set for the smaller doll). Using a flat appliqué fell-stitch, overlap the two straight sides, adjust to fit the head of the doll and sew to form a cone shape. Then, using small stitches, attach the brim of the hat to the bottom of the cone-shape.

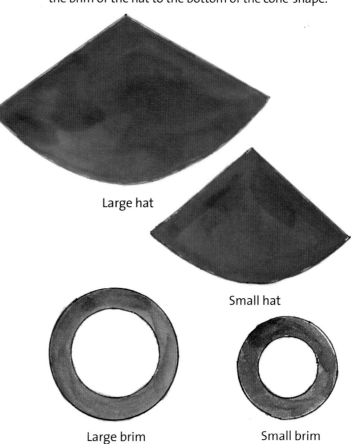

Large hat

Small hat

Large brim

Small brim

4. If you would like the top of the hat to bend, take a piece of chenille wire, 14 cm (5½ in) and bend it as indicated in the diagram. Insert it into the hat, apply glue inside the hat, and then place on the head of the doll.

Making the cloak

5. From black wool felt, cut a cloak according to the pattern. Sew a running stitch across the top of the cloak, gather slightly and knot the thread. Apply a bit of glue around the shoulders of the doll, set the cloak in place and close the front of the cloak with a stitch or two of embroidery floss.

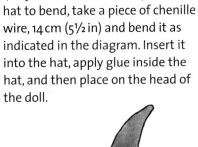

Small cloak

Large cloak

CAT

Painting the doll

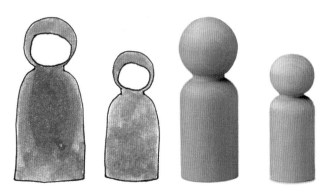

1. Using a 6 cm (2³⁄₈ in) standard people-peg for the larger cat or a 4 cm (1⁵⁄₈ in) boy-peg for a smaller cat, paint the body and head grey, leaving an unpainted oval for a face.

2. Paint a face on your doll, and if you wish, add pencil marks to indicate a few whiskers.

Making the hat

3. From grey wool felt, cut out and align front and back hat pieces (note: there are two sets of pattern pieces; one set for the larger doll and one set for the smaller doll).

4. Using two strands of matching embroidery floss, sew around the top. Then make a running stitch along the bottom edge of the back of the hat and gather slightly so that the hat will fit the contour of the head.

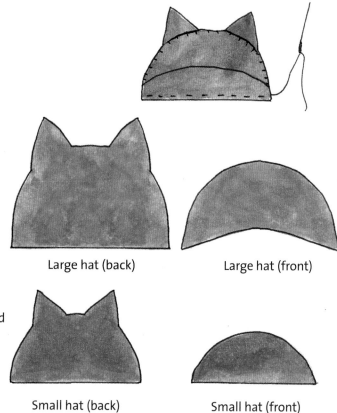

Large hat (back)

Large hat (front)

Small hat (back)

Small hat (front)

Covering the body

5. Cut the body covering according to the pattern, sew a running stitch across the top and gather slightly to fit the contour of the doll's neck and shoulders. Apply a bit of glue inside the body covering and wrap it around the doll. You can sew up the back of the doll or simply glue the ends down securely at the back.

Small body covering

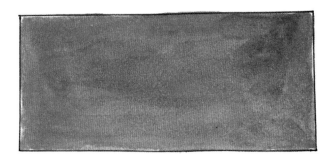

Large body covering

Finishing the doll

6. Glue the hat on the head of the doll and, if you wish, add a few stitches to tack the back of the hat down to the body covering.

GHOST

Painting the doll

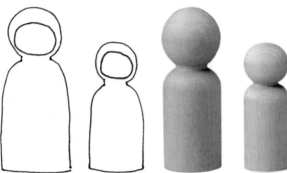

1. Using a 6 cm (2⅜ in) standard people-peg for the larger ghost or a 4 cm (1⅝ in) boy-peg for a smaller ghost, paint the body and head white, leaving an unpainted oval for a face.

2. Paint a face on your doll.

Making the hat

3. From white wool felt, cut out and align front and back hat pieces (note: there are two sets of pattern pieces; one set for the larger doll and one set for the smaller doll). Using two strands of matching embroidery floss, sew around the top and knot your thread.

4. Sew a running stitch along the bottom edge of the back of the hat, gather slightly to fit the contour of the doll's head and finish with a knot.

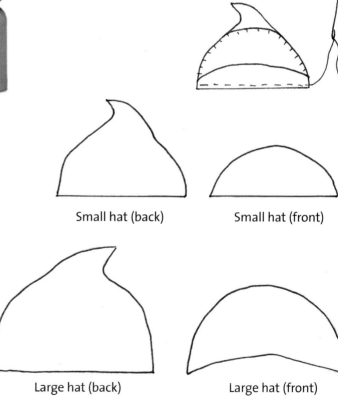

Small hat (back)   Small hat (front)

Large hat (back)   Large hat (front)

Making the cloak

5. From white wool felt, cut a cloak according to the pattern. Sew a running stitch across the top of the cloak, gather slightly and knot the thread. Sew a few stitches to tack the back edge of the hat to the top edge of the cloak, apply a bit of glue inside the hat and around the shoulders of the doll, set the cloak in place and close the front of the cloak with a stitch or two of embroidery floss.

Three little ghostesses,

Sitting on postesses,

Eating buttered toastesses,

Greasing up their fistesses,

Up to their wristesses.

Anonymous

Large cloak

Small cloak

Chapter Four

Winter

King Winter

The sky is dull and grey,
Piercing and chill the blast,
Each step resounds on the frosty ground,
Winter is come at last.
Mamma sits by the fire
Her little ones round her knees.
'How cozy we are, Mamma,' they cry,
'Tell us something, if you please.'
'Tell us about King Winter,

And about Jack Frost, his man;
We'll not be noisy or naughty at all,
But as good as ever we can.'
King Winter dwells in the North;
Far away in the Frozen Zone,
In a palace of snow he holds his court,
And sits on an icy throne.
He has cushions of course: his Queen
Made them out of her wedding gown.
Stuffing them well with snowflakes fine,
And soft as eiderdown...
His Majesty fails not to visit
Every clime that's not too hot,
To look in upon both high and low,
From the palace down to the cot.
That the King may have pleasant travel,
And no stone hurt his royal toe,
Her Majesty spreads all over the earth,
A carpet of downy snow.
Fine mirrors the King delights in:
None are finer than Jack can make:
And in matchless sheets of crystal clear
He lays them on river and lake.
The trees, all naked and drear,
He robes in the purest white,
And with icicles shining with rainbow hues,
He makes their branches bright...

Anonymous

SUPPLIES

A 5 cm (2 in) angel-peg

Watercolor paint and brushes

Wool felt: white and red

Notched felting needle, grey or white wool roving and a thick foam block

Embroidery floss and needles

Tracing paper or a photocopy of patterns

Fabric scissors

A pencil

Glue

Painting the doll

1. Paint hair and eyes on a 5 cm (2 in) angel-peg.

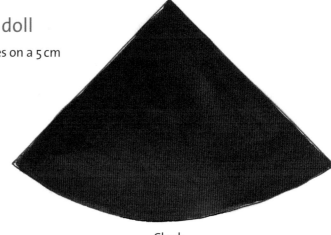

Cloak

Dressing the doll

2. Cut the tunic, cloak and belt pieces from felt. Glue the tunic over the front of the doll's body, add a bit of embroidery to the belt if you wish (I used a simple couching stitch) and then secure the belt in place with glue.

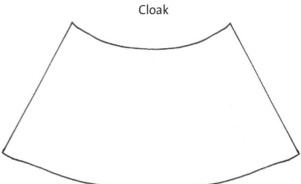

Tunic

Belt

3. To finish dressing your doll, fold the point of the cloak down 2 cm (¾ in) and tack down with a stitch of matching thread. Wrap the cloak around the back and sides of the doll and glue in place.

Adding a beard

4. To create a beard for your doll, take a few wisps of wool roving and fold the fibers in half. Place your fibers on a piece of thick foam, give them a few stabs across the folded area with your felting-needle and then, with the tip of your needle, start pulling in stray fibers from the sides and over the top. Keep stabbing and pulling in bits of stray fiber until you have a more densely felted area at the top and wisps of unfelted beard hanging down. Finally, trim your beard across the top (if necessary) and sides to neaten things up. You can also trim and shape the beard along the bottom edge, if you wish. When you are satisfied with the shape of the beard, glue it onto the lower portion of the face of your doll.

Alternatively, if you don't want to needle-felt a beard, you could use a few wisps of unfelted roving or bits of yarn to create a beard for your doll. And yet another way to make a beard would be to cut a small piece of brown, grey or black felt into shape and glue it to the face of your doll.

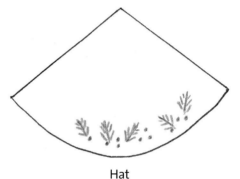

Hat

Making the hat

5. Cut out the hat according to the pattern and add embroidery according to the diagram.

6. Overlap the straight sides and adjust to fit the head of the doll. Then, using an appliqué fell-stitch, sew up the back of the hat and glue onto the head of the doll.

Angels

Oh, where do you come from, you little flakes of snow?

Falling, softly falling, on the earth below...

On the trees and on the bushes, on the mountains afar,

Tell me snowflakes, do you come from where the angels are?

Anonymous.
From page 119, *Festivals, Family and Food*, Hawthorn Press

As the year draws to a close and the days grow darker, the souls of many yearn for light and turn toward matters of the spirit. Various traditions embrace angels as guardians, messengers, embodiments of spirit which can bring us through dark days and back into light.

SUPPLIES

4 cm (1⅝ in) boy-pegs

5 cm (2 in) angel-peg

Watercolor paint and brushes

Wool felt: white and pale blue

Matching embroidery floss, gold thread and needles

Chenille wire (wire pipe-cleaner) in silver

A tiny silver bell

Tracing paper or a photocopy of patterns

Fabric scissors

A ruler

A pencil

Glue

WHITE AND SILVER ANGEL

Painting the doll

1. Paint hair and a face on a 4 cm (1⅝ in) boy-peg.

2. Paint the body of the doll white.

Creating the halo

3. Using a short length of silver pipe-cleaner (9 cm, 3½ in) twist into the shape indicated by the diagram to create a halo.

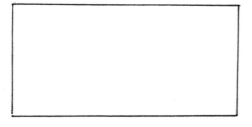

Cloak

Wings

Dressing the doll

4. Cut wing and cloak pieces according to the patterns. Sew a running stitch along the top of the cloak, gather slightly to fit the contour of the doll's neck and knot the thread.

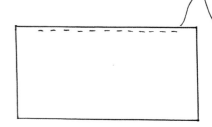

5. Place the rounded pipe-cleaner halo on top of the doll's head with the straight piece of pipe-cleaner running down the back of the head/neck (bending the back piece of wire slightly to conform to the contour of the head will help the halo stay in position). Then glue the cloak around the shoulders of the doll; the end of the pipe-cleaner should now be firmly glued inside the back of the cloak. Close the front of the cloak with a stitch or two of embroidery floss and add a tiny silver star or other ornament if you wish.

Adding wings

6. Glue the wings to the back of the doll.

BLUE AND SILVER ANGEL

Painting the doll

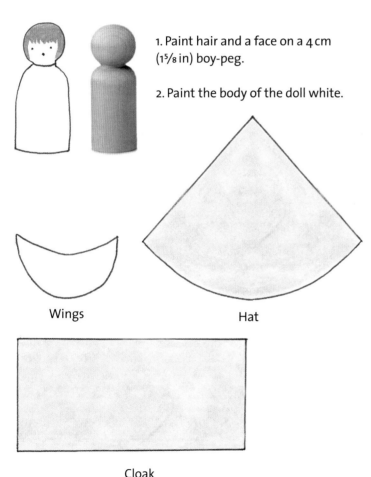

1. Paint hair and a face on a 4 cm (1⅝ in) boy-peg.

2. Paint the body of the doll white.

Wings

Hat

Cloak

Dressing the doll

3. Cut wing and cloak pieces according to the pattern. Sew a running stitch along the top of the cloak, gather slightly to fit the contour of the doll's neck and knot the thread. Then glue the cloak around the shoulders of the doll and close the front of the cloak with a stitch or two of embroidery floss. You may add a tiny silver star or other ornament if you wish...

Making the hat

4. Cut the hat according to the pattern, overlap the straight sides and adjust to fit the doll's head. Using an appliqué fell-stitch, sew up the back of the hat.

5. Then, twist one end of a 13 cm (5 in) length of silver pipe-cleaner into a circle which will fit loosely around the base of the hat. Arrange the pipe-cleaner with the straight end up inside the hat and the loop outside the hat around the base. With a few stitches, tack the base of the felt hat to the loop of silver pipe-cleaner and then glue the hat onto the head of the doll.

Adding wings

6. Stitch a tiny silver bell to the tip of the hat and glue wings onto the back of the doll.

GOLDEN STAR ANGEL

Painting the doll

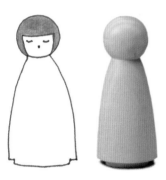

1. Paint hair and a face on a 5 cm (2 in) angel-peg.

2. Paint the body of the doll white.

Adding Embroidery

3. Cut out pieces according to the patterns: two halo pieces, two wing pieces and one cloak. Embroider stars around the halo and along the edges of the cloak. Add daisy stitches around the curved edge of the wings if you wish. Once you are finished with the embroidery, glue the second halo piece to the back of the embroidered halo to hide the back of the stitches. Glue the second wing-piece to the back of the embroidered wings to hide the back of the stitches in the same way.

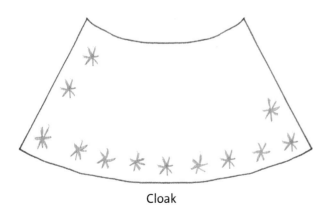

Cloak

Halo (cut 2)

Wings (cut 2)

Dressing the doll and adding wings

4. Apply glue inside the embroidered cloak, wrap around the doll and secure the front with a few stitches of embroidery floss.

5. Glue the halo to the back of the doll's head and the wings to the back of the cloak.

A Nativity Scene

The first good joy that Mary had
It was the joy of one.
The first rejoice that Mary had
Was to see her new born son.

To see her new born son good man,
And blessed may he be.
Sing Father, Son and Holy Ghost,
To all eternity.

From *The Seven Rejoices of Mary,* Traditional

SUPPLIES

5 cm (2 in) angel-pegs

A 3 cm (1³⁄₁₆ in) baby/bee-shape peg

Watercolor paint and brushes

Wool felt in various colors

Matching embroidery floss and needles

Embellishments such as beads, sequins and feathers

A notched felting needle, a thick foam block and wool roving: grey and brown

Half a walnut shell

Tracing paper or a photocopy of patterns

Beeswax polish (optional)

Fabric scissors

A pencil

Glue

MARY

Painting the doll

Hood front

Hood back

1. Paint hair and a face on a 5 cm (2 in) angel-peg.

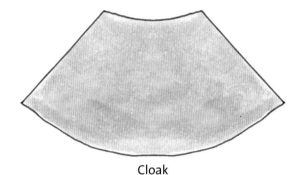

Cloak

2. Paint the body of the doll red and (optional) rub with beeswax polish.

Making the cloak

3. From blue wool felt, cut out pattern pieces for hood and cloak. Match the curved tops of the front and back pieces of the hood and, using a blanket stitch, sew over the top. Tack the back of the hood to the top of the cloak and glue onto the doll.

JOSEPH AND THE SHEPHERDS

Painting the dolls

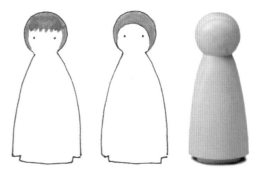

1. Paint hair and eyes on 5 cm (2 in) angel-pegs.

2. Paint the bodies of the dolls in earthy, neutral colors (I painted Joseph grey and the shepherd brown). Rub with beeswax polish (optional).

Making the cloaks

3. Cut cloaks from wool felt in earthy colors (I used brown felt for Joseph's cloak and green for the shepherd). Fold the point of the cloaks down 2 cm (¾ in) and tack down with a stitch of matching thread. Wrap the cloak around the back and sides of the doll and glue in place.

Adding beards

4. Take a few wisps of wool roving and fold the fibers in half. Place your fibers on a piece of thick foam, give them a few stabs across the folded area with your felting-needle and then, with the tip of your needle, start pulling in the fibers from the sides and over the top. Keep stabbing and pulling in bits of fiber until you have a more densely felted area at the top and wisps of unfelted beard hanging down. Finally, trim your beard across the top (if necessary) and sides to neaten things up. You can also trim and shape the beard along the bottom edge, if you wish. When you are satisfied with the shape of the beard, glue it onto the lower portion of the face of your doll.

Alternatively, if you don't want to needle-felt a beard, you could use a few wisps of unfelted roving or bits of yarn to create a beard. You could also cut a small piece of brown, grey or black felt into shape and glue it on the face of your doll.

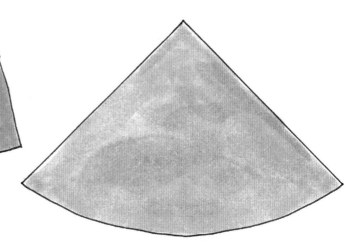

Cloak

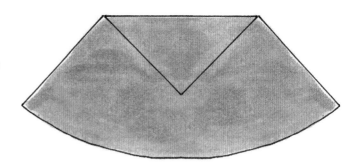

Making a staff

5. I created the shepherd's staff from heavy-gauge floral wire wrapped in brown paper and stitched it to his cloak.

MELCHIOR

Painting the doll

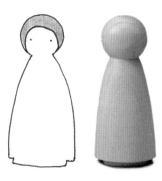

1. Paint hair and a face on a 5 cm (2 in) angel-peg.

2. Paint the body of the doll blue and (optional) rub with beeswax polish.

Making the crown

3. To create the crown for Melchior cut the three pattern pieces from wool felt (Two A-pieces from blue felt and piece B from a contrasting color.) Stitch your two A-pieces together over the curved tops.

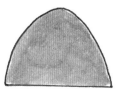

Crown A (cut 2)

Crown B

4. Take piece B and sew it around the bottom edge of the A pieces. Then tack down the points of piece A by making a small stitch near the top of each point. For a bit of sparkle, you can add a bead, sequin, glitter or a feather to the crown of your king.

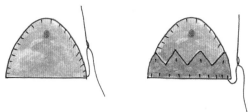

Making the cape

5. Using the pattern, cut a short cape from a color matching the trim of the crown and glue around the shoulders of the doll.

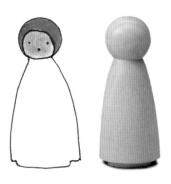

Cape

Adding a beard

6. To create a beard for Melchior, see Step 4 (page 144) instructions for Joseph and the Shepherd.

BALTHAZAR

Painting the doll

1. Paint the face brown on a 5 cm (2 in) angel-peg.

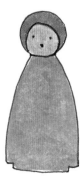

2. Paint hair and eyes.

3. Paint the body of the doll turquoise and (optional) rub with beeswax polish.

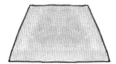

Hat (cut 2)

Making the hat

4. Cut out two hat pieces from yellow felt according to the pattern. Using a blanket stitch, sew around the top of the hat and, if you wish, you can add a bead, sequin or glitter for ornamentation. Glue the hat onto the head of the doll.

Final touch

5. Cut a strip of felt to match the hat, approximately 9 cm (3½ in). Drape it across the body of the doll over one shoulder and glue in place.

GASPAR

Painting the doll

1. Paint hair and eyes on a 5 cm (2 in) angel-peg.

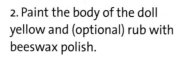

2. Paint the body of the doll yellow and (optional) rub with beeswax polish.

Making the hat

3. Cut two hat pieces from orange felt according to the pattern, sew around the top of the hat using a blanket stitch and, if you wish, add a bead, sequin, glitter or a feather for ornamentation. Glue the hat onto the head of the doll.

 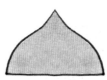

Hat (cut 2)

Adding the tunic

4. Cut two tunic pieces from orange felt according to the pattern. Glue one piece to the front of the doll and the other piece to the back so that the points meet over the shoulders of the doll.

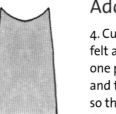

Tunic (cut 2)

THE INFANT JESUS

Painting the doll

1. Using a 3 cm (1³⁄₁₆ in) baby/bee-shape peg, paint the head and body white, leaving a small, unpainted oval for the face.

2. Paint a face on the doll.

A manger

3. Half a walnut shell makes a very nice manger.

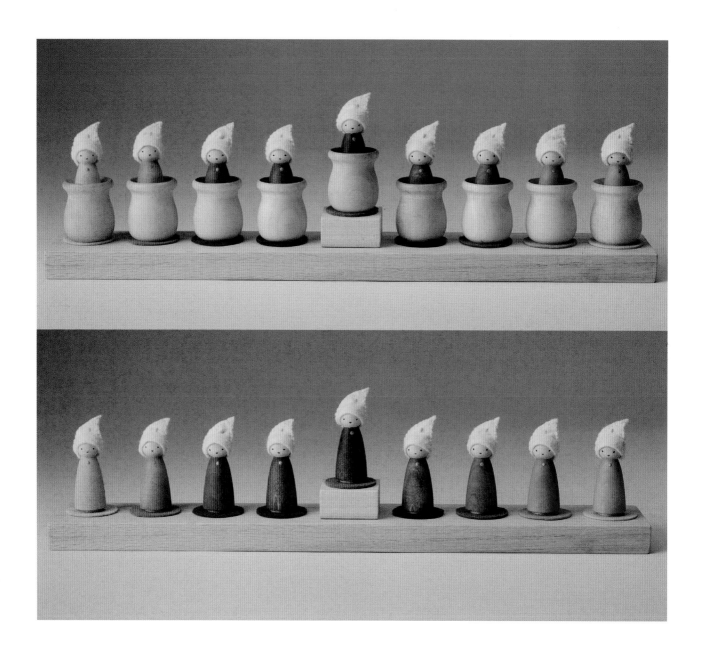

Hanukkah

SUPPLIES

Nine 5 cm (2 in) angel-pegs

*Nine wooden 'bean-pot' candle-cups, 4 cm (1⅝ in tall)

Watercolor paint and brushes

Wool felt: a rainbow of colors

Flame-colored embroidery floss and needles

Tracing paper or a photocopy of patterns

A 40.5 cm (16 in) long scrap of wood

A small wooden block, approximately 4 cm (1½ in) sq. by 2 cm (¾ in) high

Sandpaper

Beeswax polish (optional)

Fabric scissors

A ruler

A pencil

Glue

The Jewish holiday of Hanukkah, beginning on the 25th day of the Jewish lunar month of Kislev, recalls the rebuilding and rededication of the temple in Jerusalem after its destruction in 168 BCE. The flames of the Hanukkah candles symbolize joyful light after the darkness of destruction, and the lighting of the *hanukkiah* or *menorah* is central to the celebration. Hanukkah is observed over the course of eight nights, and as the holiday progresses, each night more candles are added to the *hanukkiah*.

I've created a color matching game in the shape of a *hanukkiah*, with each little figure wearing a cap in the shape of a flame to mimic the design of a candle. This would make a perfect Hanukkah gift for a young child, or if the dolls were topped with peaked gnome caps, the game could make a fun Christmas or Solstice gift.

DOLLS

Painting the dolls

1. Paint faces on nine 5 cm (2 in) angel-pegs

2. Choose nine colors of wool felt and match the colors you've chosen to nine colors in your paint-box. I chose to use a bright rainbow of colors. Paint the body of each doll a different color to match your felt and (optional) rub with beeswax polish.

Making the hats

3. From 'flame-colored' felt (yellow or orange) cut nine backs and nine fronts. Setting front on back, sew around the top using a blanket stitch.

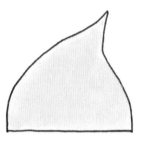

Hat back (cut 9)

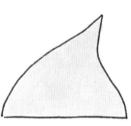

Hat front (cut 9)

4. With embroidery floss, add a stitch or two of a slightly darker color to indicate the center of the flame on each hat.

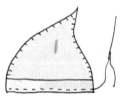

5. Along the bottom edge, at the back of each hat, add a running stitch, gather slightly to fit the contour of the heads, knot the thread and glue the hats on the heads of the dolls.

Finishing touches

6. Because the design of these little dolls is uncomplicated, there are many ways you could add additional ornamentation. For an extra bit of shine, I gilded the bases and added a gold button to the chest of each doll.

HANUKKIAH

Preparing the base

1. For the *hanukkiah* base, start with a scrap of wood and cut it so it measures 40.5 cm (16 in) long; 6.3 cm (2½ in) wide; and 2 cm (¾ in) high. (*Note: the length of the wood is most important; the width and height of your wood can be variable, as long as it accommodates the circles of felt.) Sand lightly to smooth any rough edges.

2. To add a place for the *shamash,* I used a building block, 4 cm (1½ in) square by 2 cm (¾ in) high and glued it in the center of the long wood scrap.

Adding felt circles

3. Cut a circle, 3.5 cm (1⅜ in) wide out of each color felt (for a total of nine colorful circles). Glue the circles along the length of wood at even intervals.

Adding candle cups

4. Paint the inside of each bean-pot candle-cup a different color to match each of the dolls and glue each cup onto its matching felt circle (if you prefer, you could paint the exteriors of the wooden candle-cups, instead of the interiors).

If you would like to create this game without the candle-cups, it can be made as a color-matching toy by lining up the dolls on their corresponding circles of colored felt.

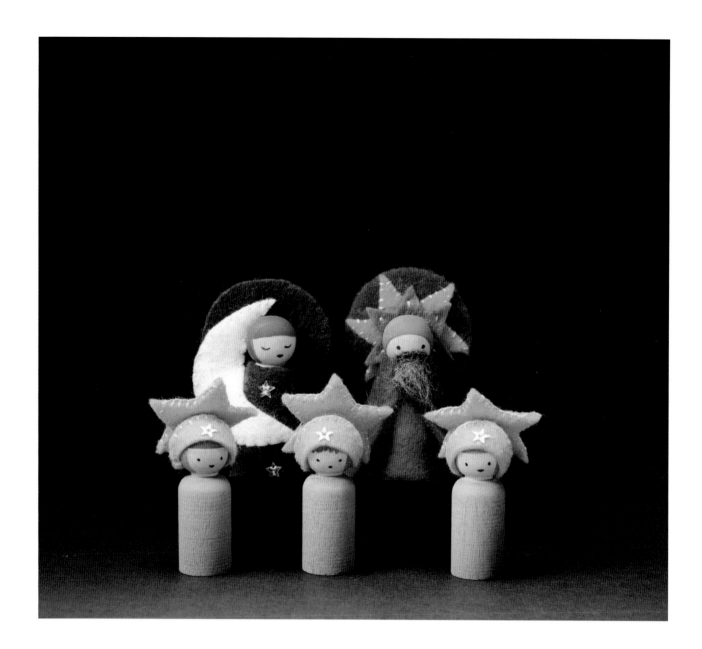

Mother Moon and Father Sun

Lovely moon, lovely moon, sailing so high,

Come to your children down from the sky.

Children dear, children dear, I cannot go;

I send my moonbeams down because I love you so.

Song, Anonymous

I learned this lullaby many years ago; the image of children calling up to their far-away mother-moon makes me feel sad, however there is a longing and gentle sweetness to this little song. I've been singing it to my children from their earliest days, and we still sing it together every time we see the moon in the sky. My little celestial figures were inspired by this lullaby, especially the tranquil Mama-Moon who sends her loving moonbeams down to all children, everywhere.

SUPPLIES

5 cm (2 in) angel-pegs

4 cm (1⅝ in) boy-pegs

Watercolor paint and brushes

Wool felt: dark and light orange, yellow, dark blue, white

Notched felting-needle, a thick foam block and wool roving: reddish-brown and orange

Matching embroidery floss and needles

Tiny star-shaped sequins

Tracing paper or a photocopy of patterns

Fabric scissors

A pencil

Glue

MAMA MOON

Painting the doll

1. Paint hair and a face on a 5 cm (2 in) angel-peg.

Dressing the doll

2. Cut out the gown according to the pattern and add star-shaped sequins or embroidered stars.

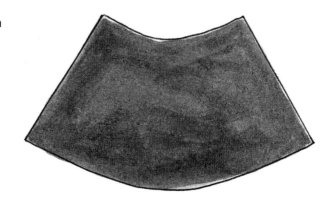

Gown

3. Apply glue down the straight edges of the gown and wrap it around the doll so that the straight edges meet at the back. For added security, I sewed up the back of the gown, but this is optional. Allow glue to dry before the next step.

Sky circle

Moon

Adding the moon

4. Cut out the moon-shape and the blue circle from wool felt according to the patterns. Pin the top third of the moon to the blue circle and then place the blue circle behind the head of the doll.

5. Bring the bottom of the moon around to the front of the doll and sew the bottom third of the moon to the front of the gown (please refer to photo of the doll to help with placement of the moon). As you sew around the side of the moon where it is not attached to the doll (or the blue circle) you can use a blanket stitch to create a decorative finished edge. Finish by sewing the top third of the moon where it is pinned to the dark blue circle.

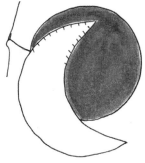

6. Tack the bottom of the blue circle to the back of the doll's gown and put a dot of glue on the back of the doll's head to hold the blue circle in place behind her.

FATHER SUN

Painting the doll

1. Paint hair and eyes on a 5 cm (2 in) angel-peg.

Dresssing the doll

2. Cut tunic and cloak pieces from wool felt according to the patterns. Glue the tunic over the front of the body of the doll then wrap the cloak around the back and glue in place.

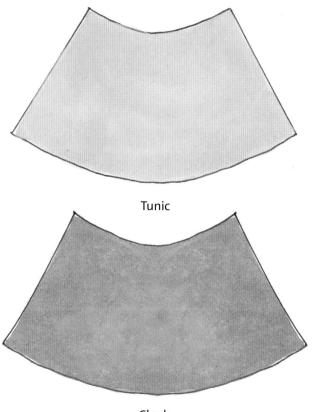

Tunic

Cloak

Making the headdress

3. Cut circle and sunburst stars from orange and yellow wool felt. Using a fell-stitch, appliqué the stars over the orange circle or tack them in place with small, embroidered stitches.

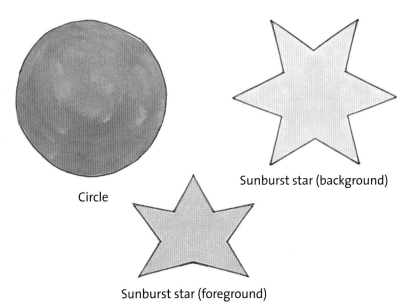

Circle

Sunburst star (background)

Sunburst star (foreground)

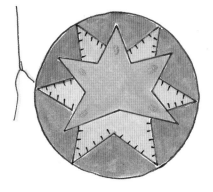

4. Glue the sunburst circle to the head of the doll (and to the back of the cloak) so that the sunburst forms a corona around the doll's head.

Adding a beard

5. To create a beard for your doll take a few wisps of wool roving (for Father Sun, I used reddish-brown roving overlaid with a wisp of orange) and fold the fibers in half. Place your fibers on a piece of thick foam, give them a few stabs across the folded area with your felting-needle and then, with the tip of your needle, start pulling in the fibers from the sides and over the top. Keep stabbing and pulling in bits of fiber until you have a more densely felted area at the top and wisps of unfelted beard hanging down. Finally, trim your beard across the top (if necessary) and sides to neaten things up. You can also trim and shape the beard along the bottom edge, if you wish. When you are satisfied with the shape of the beard, glue it onto the lower portion of the face of your doll.

Alternatively, you could use a few wisps of unfelted roving or bits of yarn to create a beard for your doll. Yet another way to make a beard would be to cut a small piece of brown, grey or black felt into shape and glue it on the face of your doll.

BABY STARS

Painting the dolls

1. Paint hair and faces on 4 cm (1⅝ in) boy-pegs.

2. Paint the bodies light blue.

Making the hats

3. From yellow wool felt, cut front and back hat pieces plus two stars per doll. Match the curved tops of the hat pieces together and sew using a blanket stitch. Tack on a little star-shaped sequin to the front or add embroidery if you wish.

4. Add a running stitch along the bottom edge of the back of the hat, gather slightly to fit the contour of the doll's head, knot the thread and glue hat onto the doll.

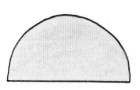

Hat back

Hat front

Star (cut 2)

5. Place two wool felt star-shapes together and sew around the edges. Glue to the back of the doll's head.

Valentine's Day

I will make you brooches and toys for your delight

Of bird song at morning and starshine at night.

I will make a palace fit for you and me,

Of green days in forests and blue days at sea.

Robert Louis Stevenson

Don't you think it would be enchanting for a child to discover one of these little Valentine friends waiting beside a plate of toast and raspberry jam on the morning of Valentine's Day?

SUPPLIES

4 cm (1⅝ in) boy-pegs

Watercolor paint and brushes

Wool felt: pink, red and white

A craft punch in the shape of tiny flowers or stars

Light card stock, pale pink or other preferred color

Silk flowers, stamens and/or tiny silk leaves

Green floral tape

Tweezers

Glue

Painting the dolls

1. Paint hair and faces on 4 cm (1⅝ in) boy-pegs.

2. Paint the bodies red or pale pink.

Adding a flower garland

3. To add a flower-garland around the head of your doll, use a craft-punch and light-weight cardstock to create tiny flowers. Pour a small puddle of glue into a paper cup (or some other type of small, disposable container), and, using tweezers, pick up a tiny flower by one petal, touch the back of the flower to the glue and place on the head of the doll. Repeat until a tiny garland of flowers is formed.

Bearing valentine hearts and bouquets

4. Cut hearts out of white, pink or red felt and attach with glue to the front of the dolls.

5. Alternatively, artificial flower stamens make perfect doll-size bouquets. To make bouquets, use floral tape to wrap the stems (you can also add a tiny silk leaf for a bit of extra color and texture). Once the stems are wrapped, simply glue the bouquets to the front of the dolls.

Breaking the Rules

In designing these dolls, I broke two of my own rules. The first is that I don't usually use paper when designing dolls; however, because the pieces are very small and securely glued they are not particularly fragile. The second rule I broke has to do with using tweezers. When I see instructions for a project so small and delicate it requires tweezers for construction, I think to myself that it must surely be quite difficult. Once I got started using the tweezers, I found it wasn't very difficult; however, when my 8-year-old wanted to add some tiny flowers to one of his dolls, he needed a bit of assistance. Still, if the idea of tracking down a pair of tweezers for this project does not appeal to you, there are many other ideas for hats and head coverings in this book which you could adapt for this project!

Chapter Five

Tell me a story

The Three Bears

Once upon a time there were three bears: a great-big papa bear, a middle-size mama bear and a tiny-wee baby bear. Together they lived in a snug cottage beneath the tall trees of a great, dark wood. One morning, mama bear set out three bowls of porridge and honey for breakfast: A great-big bowl for the great-big papa bear, a middle-sized bowl for the middle-sized mama bear and a tiny-wee bowl for the tiny-wee baby bear. But the porridge was too hot to eat so the three bears went for a walk in the woods to collect acorns and mushrooms.

While they were out, a little girl named Goldilocks happened upon the cottage. Overcome with curiosity, she peered through the windows and spied three bowls of porridge on the table. The porridge looked delicious, and suddenly, Goldilocks realized she was feeling rather hungry...

SUPPLIES

Two 6 cm (2³⁄₈ in) standard-size people-pegs

Two 4 cm (1⁵⁄₈ in) boy-pegs

Watercolor paint and brushes

Wool felt: light and dark brown plus red or another pretty color for Goldilocks' cap

Patterned paper or bright colored felt for Goldilocks' apron

Matching embroidery floss and needles

Tracing paper or a photocopy of patterns

Beeswax polish (optional)

Fabric scissors

Glue

BEARS

Painting the dolls

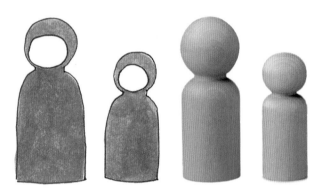

1. Using dark brown, paint the heads and bodies of two 6 cm (2³⁄₈ in) standard-size people-pegs and one 4 cm (1⁵⁄₈ in) boy-peg brown. Leave unpainted ovals or circles unpainted for the faces. Rub with beeswax polish (optional).

2. Paint a face on each of the dolls.

Making the hats

3. Cut out hat pieces from brown felt according to the patterns. Align the tops of the hats and sew using a blanket stitch.

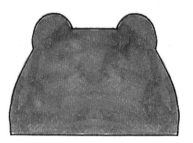

Large hat back

Large hat front

Small hat back

Small hat front

4. Add a running stitch along the bottom edge of the back of the hats, gather slightly to accommodate the contour of the dolls' heads, knot the thread and glue onto the dolls.

Finishing touches

5. Cut stomach pieces from lighter brown felt and glue onto the fronts of the dolls. Paint buttons or any additional ornamentation you wish.

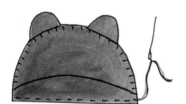

Large bear stomach   Small bear stomach

GOLDILOCKS

Painting the dolls

1. Paint hair and a face on a 4 cm (1⅝ in) boy-peg.

2. Paint the body blue.

Making the bonnet

3. Cut bonnet from red wool felt according to the pattern. Overlap the straight sides and adjust the size to fit the head of the doll. Using a flat fell-stitch, sew the two straight sides together to form a cone shape and then tack the point of the cone down at the back to form a bonnet.

Bonnet

4. If you would like to add plaits, you can make them from embroidery floss and secure them beneath the hat when you glue the hat onto the doll.

Adding an apron

5. I used paper with a red-checked pattern to create an apron for this doll, but a piece of felt, cut according to the same pattern and glued to the doll, would work equally well.

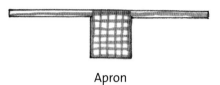

Apron

Red Riding Hood

Grandmother, what big eyes you have...

    The better to see you with, my dear.

And Grandmother, what big ears you have...

    The better to hear you with, my dear.

Grandmother, what a big nose you have...

    The better to (sniff, sniff) smell you with, my dear.

Oh, Grandmother, what big teeth you have...

    The better to eat you with, my dear!

Traditional

RED RIDING HOOD

Painting the doll

1. Paint hair and a face on a 4 cm (1⅝ in) boy-peg.

2. Paint the body ochre yellow.

Making the cloak

3. From red wool felt, cut pieces for the hood and cloak according to the patterns. Match the top of the hood pieces and sew using a blanket stitch.

4. Add a running stitch along the bottom edge at the back of the hood, gather slightly to accommodate the contour of the head and knot the thread.

Cloak

Hood (back)

Hood (front)

WOLF

Painting the doll

1. Using a 6 cm (2⅜ in) standard-size wood-people-peg, paint the body and head grey, leaving an unpainted oval for the face.

5. Add a running stitch along the top of the cloak, gather slightly and then, with a few small stitches, sew the back of the hood to the center of the cloak. Glue onto the doll.

2. Paint a face on your doll. For a slightly fierce look, use a pencil to add some eyebrows.

Making the headdress

3. Cut all pieces for the wolf's headdress from grey wool felt according to the patterns. Align the top curves of the front and back pieces. Using a blanket stitch, sew the two pieces together over the top curve.

4. Fold the snout-piece so that the stars on the pattern-piece are aligned and, using a blanket stitch, sew along the short, front, curved portion. Then position this snout piece over the front of the headdress so the snout protrudes but does not cover the face. Sew the snout piece in place.

5. Tack the ears to the sides of the headdress and glue the headdress in place.

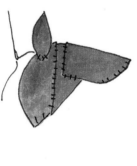

Hat (back)

Hat (front)

Snout

Ear (cut 2)

Finishing touches

6. Cut the stomach oval and two tail-pieces for the wolf from lighter grey wool felt. Glue oval to the front of the wolf. Using a running stitch, sew the two tail-pieces together according to the diagram, splay the seam open at the bottom and glue the splayed area to the back of the wolf.

Tail (cut 2)

Stomach

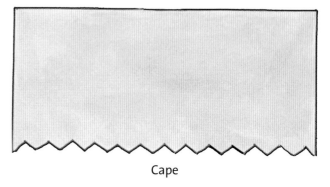

Cape

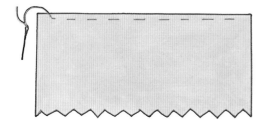

7. For the wolf masquerading as Grandmother, cut the front and back headdress pieces from peach colored felt, sew the ears and snout on per the directions above. Then cut a narrow length of pink felt with pinking shears and glue it over the top of the cap, in front of the ears. Cut a cape from pink felt according to the pattern, sew a running stitch across the top and gather slightly so that it fits around the shoulders of the doll. Glue in place and add a stitch or two of matching embroidery floss to close the front.

THE HELPFUL WOODSMAN

Painting the doll

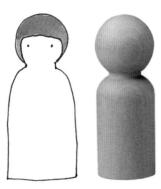

1. Paint hair and eyes on a 6 cm (2⅜ in) standard-size wood-people-peg.

2. Paint shirt, trousers and a belt on the body of the doll.

Adding a cape

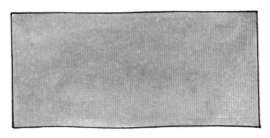

Cape

3. Cut the cape from green felt according to the pattern, sew a running stitch across the top and gather slightly so that it fits around the shoulders of the doll. Glue in place and add a stitch or two of matching embroidery floss to close the front.

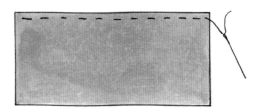

Making the hat

4. Cut two hat pieces from green felt according to the pattern. Using a blanket stitch, sew over the top of the hat, then fold the back of the hat up 6 mm (¼ in) and tack in place with a stitch or two. Glue onto the head of the doll with the point at the front and the folded section in back.

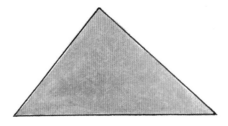

Hat (cut 2)

Adding a beard

5. To create a beard for your Woodsman, take a few wisps of wool roving and fold the fibers in half. Place your fibers on a piece of thick foam, give them a few stabs across the folded area with your felting-needle and then, with the tip of your needle, start pulling in the fibers from the sides and over the top. Keep stabbing and pulling in bits of fiber until you have a more densely felted area at the top and

wisps of unfelted beard hanging down. Finally, trim your beard across the top (if necessary) and sides to neaten things up. You can also trim and shape the beard along the bottom edge, if you wish. When you are satisfied with the shape of the beard, glue it onto the lower portion of the face of your doll.

Alternatively, if you don't want to needle-felt a beard, you could use a

few wisps of unfelted roving or bits of yarn to create a beard for your doll. And yet another way to make a beard would be to cut a small piece of brown, grey or black felt into shape and glue it on the face of your doll.

Hansel and Gretel

Nibble, nibble little mouse,

Who's that nibbling on my house?

Traditional

SUPPLIES

One 6 cm (2³⁄₈ in) standard-size people-peg

Two 4 cm (1⁵⁄₈ in) boy-peg

Watercolor paint and brushes

Wool felt: light and dark brown, black and light blue

A bit of grey wool yarn

Matching embroidery floss and needles

Tracing paper or a photocopy of the patterns

Fabric scissors

Glue

HANSEL

Painting the doll

1. Paint hair and face on a 4 cm (1⅝ in) boy-peg.

2. Paint the top of the body blue and the bottom half green. Rub with a beeswax polish (optional).

Adding braces

3. Cut braces from dark brown felt according to the pattern and embroider a little star on the front. Glue the belt portion around the middle of the body and the braces over the shoulders, crossed at the back.

Braces

GRETEL

Painting the doll

1. Paint hair and a face on a 4 cm (1⁵⁄₈ in) boy-peg.

2. Paint the body green. Rub with a beeswax polish (optional).

Apron

Making the bonnet

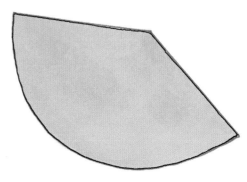

Bonnet

3. Cut bonnet from blue wool felt according to the pattern, overlap the straight sides and adjust size to fit the head of the doll. Using a fell-stitch, sew the straight sides together to form a cone shape and then tack the point of the cone down at the back to form a bonnet. If you would like to add plaits, you can make them from embroidery floss and secure them beneath the hat when you the glue the hat onto the doll.

Adding an apron

4. Cut an apron from dark brown felt, embroider a star on the front and glue in place.

WITCH

Painting the doll

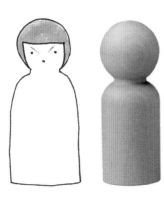

1. Paint hair and a face on a 6 cm (2³⁄₈ in) standard-size people-peg. For a fierce look, I used a pencil to add eyebrows.

2. Paint the body of the doll dark grey.

Making the cloak

3. From brown wool felt, cut a cloak according to the pattern. Sew a running stitch across the top of the cloak, gather gently and knot the thread. Apply a bit of glue around the shoulders of the doll, set the cloak in place and close the front of the cloak with a stitch or two of embroidery floss.

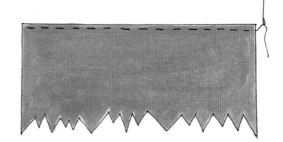

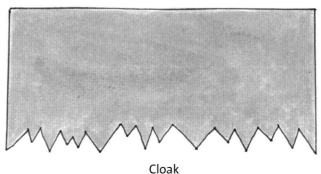

Cloak

Making the hat

4. From black wool felt, cut out the piece for the witch's hat and, using a fell-stitch, sew up the back to form a cone.

5. If you would like to add hair, you can secure the ends of a few strands of grey yarn beneath the hat when you glue the hat onto the head of the doll.

Hat

6. If you would like the top of the hat to bend, take a small piece of chenille wire 14 cm (5½ in) and bend it as indicated in the diagram. Insert it into the hat, apply glue inside the hat and then place on the head of the doll.

RESOURCE GUIDE FOR PURCHASING MATERIALS

England

MOTHER GOOSE
10a Market Street
Nailsworth
Stroud
Gloucestershire, GL6 0BX
Tel: +44 (01453) 298725
www.mothergooseonline.co.uk

MYRIAD NATURAL TOYS AND
CRAFTS
Old Stable
Nine Yews
Cranborne
Dorset, BH21 5PW
Tel: +44 (01725) 517085 or
+44 (01725) 517040
www.myriadonline.co.uk

Wooden doll bases (conical figures), wool felt,
needle-felting materials, waxed kite paper,
paints and colored pencils.

Australia

EPOCHE
77 Monbulk Road
Kallista
Victoria 3791
Tel: +61 (03) 9755 1952
www.epoche.com.au

Natural crafting supplies.

MORNING STAR CRAFTS
Tel: +61 (03) 5985 6797
www.morningstarcrafts.com.au

Wool felt, needle-felting supplies, wooden
doll bases, waxed kite paper, watercolor
paints, colored pencils and natural beeswax.

WINTERWOOD TOYS
9 Colman Road
Warranwood
Victoria 3134
Tel: +61 (03) 9879 0426
www.winterwoodtoys.com

Wooden doll bases, wool felt, needle-felting
supplies, waxed kite paper, paints and
colored pencils.

Canada

BEAR DANCE CRAFTS
Tel: +1 (250) 353 2220
www.beardancecrafts.com

Wooden doll bases, wool felt and needle-
felting supplies.

BEAR WOODS SUPPLY CO., INC
Tel: +1 (800) 565 5066
www.woodparts.ca

MAPLEROSE
265 Baker Street
Nelson, BC
V1L 4H4
Tel: +1 (250) 352 5729

www.maplerose.ca

Wooden doll bases, wool felt and needle-
felting supplies, waxed kite paper, paints and
colored pencils, beeswax.

USA

BELLA LUNA TOYS
Tel: +1 (888) 438 1299
www.bellalunatoys.com

Wooden doll bases, wool felt and needle-
felting supplies, waxed kite paper, paints and
colored pencils, beeswax.

CASEY'S WOOD
Tel: +1 (800) 452 2739
www.caseyswood.com

Doll bases (peg people), candle cups, and an
assortment of other wonderful and useful
wooden pieces. Note: Casey's Wood will ship
their wood products internationally.

A CHILD'S DREAM COME TRUE
214-A Cedar Street
Sandpoint
Idaho 83864
Tel: +1 (208) 255 1664
www.achildsdream.com

Wool felt, needle-felting supplies, waxed kite
paper, paints and colored pencils, wooden doll
bases.

ACKNOWLEDGEMENTS

NOVA NATURAL
Tel: +1 (877) 668 2111
www.novanatural.com

Wool felt, needle-felting supplies, waxed kite paper, paints and colored pencils, beeswax.

WOODWORKS LTD
4521 Anderson Boulevard
Haltom City
TX 76117
Tel: +1 (800) 722 0311 or
+1 (817) 581 5230
www.craftparts.com

Wooden peg doll bases and a wide assortment of other wooden shapes and pieces. Note: Woodworks will ship their wood products internationally.

Author's Acknowledgements
Thank you to Lev for coming down from the stars to join our family and for taking long afternoon sleeps; to Samuel for the afternoons you sat with me at the table painting dolls, and because you are my beautiful boy; to Paul for sharing this wonderful life with me, for seeing the magic and photographing it, too; to my brother Jesse Milden, for your patience and wit; to my parents, Martin and Sandra Milden, for your unconditional love and giddy joy when I revealed this project to you; to my mother-in-law Rose Bloom for more giddy joy and support for this project; to Pam Leffler, Najia Saidi, Caroline Spinali, and Denise Tyree for the afternoons you welcomed my big boy into your homes so I could have time to prepare this manuscript; to Marilyn Scott-Waters for offering encouragement from the very beginning when I needed it most; to Shannon Morris, Melissa Polk, Caroline Spinali, Anna Branford and Clare Borchers for your thoughtful suggestions and endless support; to Kazuko Yamashiro for your advice regarding Japanese traditions; to Joanne Konezny for your love and friendship; to Adrian, Alyse, Arabella, Grayson, Imriel, Karina, Karissa, Kotoko, Logan, Lupine, Reese, Riley, Sage, Samuel, and Ziggy for offering me your inspirational dolls; to Claire Percival for your communication and facilitation, without which, this book would not be possible; to Lucy Guenot for making everything look gorgeous; and finally, to Martin Large for having faith in this project and allowing me the honor of sharing tiny doll magic.

Margaret Bloom lives with her family in a little cottage beneath the great oak trees of Northern California. She has a Master's Degree in Counseling Psychology, has worked as a professional puppeteer and she loves making peg dolls with her children. It gives her the greatest joy to inspire children and families everywhere to create, to play and to dream...

www.webloomhere.blogspot.com

Thank you to Shannon Morris for the clothespeg dolls on page 9. Thank you to Melissa Polk and Rachel Wolf for the peg dolls on page 10.

Thank you to M. B. Goffstein for kind permission to use the excerpt from *Goldie the Dollmaker* on page 2.

Thank you to Anita Lobel for kind permission to use the excerpt from *Under a Mushroom* on page 97, and thank you also to Paul King for kind permission to use his *Acorn* poem on page 95.

Stockists

If you have difficulties ordering Hawthorn Press books from a bookshop, you can order direct from our website **www.hawthornpress.com** or the following distributors:

Hawthorn Press

UK
BookSource: tel +44 (0141) 643 3950
email: orders@booksource.net
www.booksource.net

USA
Steiner Books: tel (800) 856 8664
email: service@steinerbooks.org
www.steinerbooks.org

AUSTRALIA AND NEW ZEALAND
Footprint Books: tel +61 (02) 9997 3973
email: info@footprint.com.au
www.footprint.com.au

Waldorf Books: tel (800) 472 4610
email: info@waldorfbooks.com
www.waldorfbooks.com

....

Other Books by Hawthorn Press

Books can be ordered direct from **www.hawthornpress.com**

Therapeutic Storytelling
SUSAN PERROW
ISBN 978-1-907359-15-6
272pp, 234 x 159mm

Healing Stories for Challenging Behaviour
SUSAN PERROW
ISBN: 978-1-903458-78-5
320pp, 234 x 156mm

Making Waldorf Dolls
MARICRISTIN SEALEY
ISBN 978-1-903458-58-7
160pp, 246 x 189mm

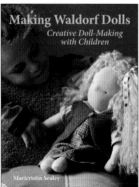

Puppet Theatre
MAIJA BARIC
ISBN 978-1-903458-72-3
96pp, 210 x 260mm